STUDY GUIDE

for use with

FINANCIAL ACCOUNTING

STUDY GUIDE

for use with

FINANCIAL ACCOUNTING

SECOND EDITION

WALTER B. MEIGS, Ph.D., C.P.A.

Professor of Accounting
University of Southern California

A. N. MOSICH, Ph.D., C.P.A.

Professor of Accounting
University of Southern California

ROBERT F. MEIGS, D.B.A.

Associate Professor of Accounting
California State University, San Diego

McGRAW-HILL BOOK COMPANY

New York   St. Louis   San Francisco   Auckland   Düsseldorf   Johannesburg   Kuala Lumpur   London
Mexico   Montreal   New Delhi   Panama   Paris   São Paulo   Singapore   Sydney   Tokyo   Toronto

STUDY
GUIDE
for use with
FINANCIAL
ACCOUNTING

ISBN 0-07-041295-2

567890BABA79876

This book was set in Alphavers Book by John C. Meyer & Son.
The editors were J. S. Dietrich, Michael Elia, and Annette Hall;
the cover was designed by Nicholas Krenitsky;
the production supervisor was Thomas J. LoPinto.
George Banta Company, Inc., was printer and binder.

CONTENTS

TO THE STUDENT

This self-study guide is designed for your use as a student taking your first course in accounting at either the undergraduate or the graduate level. It is prepared to accompany *Financial Accounting,* Second Edition, by Meigs, Mosich, and Meigs. However, it can be used effectively with other introductory accounting texts. The key purposes of this study guide are:

1 To help you in ***mastering the material*** as you initially study each chapter.
2 To ***summarize the essential points*** in each chapter and to ***test your knowledge*** with a series of objective questions and exercises, thus making it possible for you to ***review the material quickly*** from time to time, particularly before examinations.
3 To make the study of accounting ***more enjoyable and less tedious*** for you. This is accomplished by presenting an informal and concise summary of each chapter, followed by three groups of objective questions and some short exercises. The answers to these questions and exercises are provided in the back of the study guide ***in order to give you immediate feedback and point out areas that need additional attention.***

The manner in which each student uses this study guide may differ. However, we recommend the following approach:

1 Study the chapter in your textbook.
2 Read the ***Highlights of the Chapter*** section of the study guide. If you encounter any statements that you do not understand, refer to the textbook for a more detailed discussion of the topic.
3 Work the questions and exercises in the ***Test Yourself*** section of the study guide, and compare your answers and solutions with those provided in the back of the guide. This will show you how well you really understand the material contained in the related chapter of your textbook. Again, if you find something you do not understand, refer to your text for a thorough discussion of the subject.
4 Work the problems assigned as homework in your text.

Once you have mastered the material in this manner, rereading the ***Highlights of the Chapter*** section of the study guide will assist you in quickly reviewing the material before examinations.

WALTER B. MEIGS
A. N. MOSICH
ROBERT F. MEIGS

STUDY
GUIDE
for use with
FINANCIAL
ACCOUNTING

ONE

ACCOUNTING THE BASIS FOR BUSINESS DECISIONS

HIGHLIGHTS OF THE CHAPTER

1 The basic purpose of accounting is to provide financial information about a business enterprise or any other economic entity. This information is needed internally by managers and also by outsiders such as bankers, other creditors, investors, and certain government agencies. In short, anyone who must make *decisions* regarding a business enterprise has need of *accounting information.*

2 Most businesses enter into so many different transactions every year that a complete list of these transactions would be too long to be useful to decision makers. An accounting system creates *useful* information by (a) *recording* business events as they occur, (b) *classifying* these events into related groups, and (c) *summarizing* this information into concise reports called *financial statements.*

3 Financial statements show the financial position of the business at a given date and also the operating results which caused it to arrive at this position.

4 *Bookkeeping* refers to the mechanical aspects of recording and classifying transactions, and is but a small part of the field of accounting. *Accounting* includes the design of the financial information system, preparation of financial statements, development of budgets, cost studies, tax consulting, and the *analysis* and *interpretation* of accounting information to assist decision makers in making *informed* decisions.

5 Careers in accounting may be divided into three broad areas: (a) the public accounting profession, (b) private accounting, and (c) governmental accounting.

6 Public accounting is practiced by *certified public accountants,* called CPAs. CPAs are granted a license to practice by the state, and perform professional accounting services for clients for a fee. These services include:

a *Auditing* An audit is an investigation of a company's accounting system to determine that the financial statements *present fairly* its financial position and operating results. All large corporations and many small companies are audited annually by a CPA firm.

b *Tax services* Taxes often play an important role in financial decisions. CPA firms offer "tax planning" services to minimize the impact of taxes on their clients, and also assist in the preparation of their clients' tax returns.

c *Management advisory services* CPA firms may become familiar with their clients' problems and be able to recommend corrective action. This service is actually *management consulting.*

7 *Private accounting* refers to the work of accountants employed directly by private industry. The functions of accountants in private industry include:

a *Design of accounting systems* Although most business concerns follow the same basic accounting principles, each firm will require its own individually tailored accounting system.

b *Cost accounting* This is the specialized field of determining the cost of manufacturing a product or performing a specific process.

c *Budgeting* A budget is a plan of financial operations for the future. The budget helps management to set goals, and then to measure actual performance relative to these goals.

d *Tax accounting* Tax specialists play as important a role in private accounting as they do in public accounting.

e *Internal auditing* Internal auditors are responsible for seeing that the objectives of a company are being carried out efficiently in all departments.

Unlike CPAs, internal auditors are **not** responsible for determining the fairness of annual financial statements.

f Management accounting Managers of a business enterprise require much specialized information about the business on a day-to-day basis. Filling these special information needs of managers is the job of the managerial accountant.

8 Governmental accounting includes many specialized areas such as monitoring regulated industries, auditing tax returns, and preparing budgets for governmental agencies. Two important governmental agencies using accounting information are:

a Internal Revenue Service The IRS processes the federal income tax returns filed by individuals and corporations.

b Securities and Exchange Commission The SEC reviews and approves the financial disclosure by corporations which offer their securities for sale to the public.

9 Two primary objectives of most business concerns are to make a profit and remain solvent. Being **solvent** means having the cash to pay debts on time. The accounting system is the means by which profitability and solvency are measured.

10 Steps taken to ensure the reliability of accounting information and to safeguard the resources of a business against waste, fraud, or inefficient use are called the system of **internal control.**

11 Accounting information is gathered for specific accounting entities. An accounting entity is any economic unit which enters into business transactions. The business activity of a specific entity should be regarded as separate from other business activities of its owners.

12 A **balance sheet** is the financial statement showing the financial condition of a business at a particular date. It consists of a list of the company's assets, liabilities, and owners' equity.

13 The three most common forms of business organizations are single proprietorships, partnerships, and corporations.

14 Assets are economic resources owned by a business, such as land, buildings, and cash. Assets are valued on a balance sheet at their **cost,** rather than at current market prices, because cost is more factual and can be more objectively determined than current market value. Another reason for valuing assets at cost is that a business is assumed to be a "going concern" that will keep and use such assets as land and buildings rather than sell them.

15 Liabilities are debts. Either borrowing money or buying on credit will create a liability. Liabilities represent the claims of **creditors** to the resources of the business. Examples of liabilities are accounts payable and notes payable.

16 Owners' equity represents the owners' claim to the resources of a business enterprise. Owners' equity in a corporation is called **stockholders' equity.** It is increased by (a) investments of cash or other assets by persons who receive shares of stock in exchange, and are called stockholders and (b) profitable operation of the business. Stockholders' equity is decreased by (a) the payment of dividends to stockholders and (b) unprofitable operation of the business.

17 The "accounting equation" is **Assets = Liabilities + Owners' Equity.** The listing of assets shows us what things the business owns; the listing of liabilities and owners' equity tells us who supplied these resources to the business and how much each group supplied.

18 You should become familiar with the effects of various transactions upon a balance sheet.

a Purchasing an asset for cash is merely trading one kind of asset for another. Total assets will not change.

b Purchasing an asset on credit will cause total assets to increase because additional resources are being acquired, and none is being given up. However, total liabilities will increase by the same amount.

c Paying a liability with cash will cause both total assets and total liabilities to decrease.

TEST YOURSELF
ON THIS INTRODUCTORY CHAPTER

True or False

For each of the following statements, circle the T or the F to indicate whether the statement is true or false.

 T F **1** The basic purpose of accounting is to provide financial information to economic decision makers.

 T F **2** Bookkeeping is only a small part of the field of accounting and probably the simplest part.

 T F **3** The most useful financial statement would be a detailed list of every business transaction in which the business enterprise has been involved.

 T **F** **4** Financial statements are confidential documents made available only to the top management of a business enterprise.

T F 5 The CPA is an independent professional person and is not an employee of the company for which he performs an annual audit.

T F 6 All large corporations, such as those listed on the New York Stock Exchange, are audited each year by a CPA firm, thus adding credibility and reliability to their financial reports.

T F 7 The chief accounting officer of a corporation is usually called the controller.

T **F** 8 A budget for a business enterprise is always prepared by the CPA firm conducting the annual audit.

T F 9 A business may be profitable, but not solvent.

T **F** 10 A business may be solvent, but not profitable.

T **F** 11 Assets are valued on the balance sheet at current liquidation values to show how much cash would be realized if the business went broke.

T **F** 12 The purchase of a building for cash will cause total assets to increase.

T F 13 The payment of a liability will not affect total assets, but will cause total liabilities to decrease.

T F 14 In the balance sheet of a single proprietorship, any increase in capital earned through profitable operations and retained in the business is added to the capital originally invested, and a single figure is shown for the owner's capital.

T **F** 15 State laws require corporations to show capital stock and retained earnings separately on the balance sheet.

Completion Statements

Fill in the necessary words or amounts to complete the following statements:

1 Two major financial statements are the _Balance Sheet_ and the _income sheet_.

2 The three basic steps in the accounting process are (a) _recording_ transactions, (b) _putting_ these events into groups, and (c) _combining_ the information in financial statements.

3 The accounting equation states that _assets_ = _Liabilities_ + _Capital_.

4 The heading of a balance sheet should include (a) _Company_, (b) _date_ , and (c) _title_ .

5 An investigation of the accounting system of a business to determine the fairness of the firm's financial statement is called an _audit_ .

6 The governmental agency which reviews and approves the financial disclosure by companies which offer their securities to the public is the _S.E.C._ .

7 The steps taken to ensure the reliability of the accounting information and to safeguard the assets of the firm against waste, fraud, or inefficient use make up the system of _Internal control_ .

8 Two primary objectives of most business concerns are (a) making a _profit_ and (b) remaining _solvent_ .

9 Since the claims of _creditors_ have priority over those of the _owners_ of a business, the owners' equity is called a _residual_ claim. _stockholders_

10 Land advertised for sale at $90,000 was purchased for $80,000 cash by a development company. For property tax purposes, the property was assessed by the county at $25,000. The development firm intended to sell the property in parcels for a total of $150,000. The land would appear on the balance sheet of the development company among the _Land_ at a value of $_80,000_ .

11 On December 15, Shadow Mountain Golf Course had a contractor install a $90,000 sprinkler system. Since no payment to the contractor was required until the following month, the transaction was not recorded in December and was not reflected in any way in the December 31 balance sheet. Indicate for each of the following elements of the balance sheet whether the amounts were overstated, understated, or correct. Total assets _understated_ , total liabilities _understated_ owners' equity _overstated correct_

12 The owners' equity in a business comes from two sources: (a) _the owners_ and (b) _profits_ .

13 A transaction which causes total liabilities to increase, but has no effect on owners' equity, must cause total assets to _increase_ .

14 Retained earnings represent the total earnings (profits) of a business which have not been paid out as _dividends_ to the _stockholders_ .

Multiple Choice

Choose the best answer for each of the following questions and enter the identifying letter in the space provided.

___*b*___ **1** Which of the following best describes the nature of an asset?

a Something with a ready market value.

b An economic resource, which will provide some future benefits, owned by a business.

c Tangible property (something with physical form) owned by a business.

d The amount of the owners' investment in a business.

X ___*a*___ **2** A budget is defined as:

a The process of determining the cost of producing a particular product or of performing a particular business operation.

b The division of cash on hand at year-end among the various objectives for which it must be disbursed.

c A plan of financial operations for some future period expressed in accounting terms.

d The assessment of penalties and distribution of bonuses to supervisors whose performance has fallen below or has exceeded predetermined standards. *d*

X ___*d*___ **3** The principal reason for an annual audit of a business corporation by a firm of certified public accountants (CPAs) is:

a To obtain an independent expert opinion on the fairness and dependability of the financial statements prepared by the company and distributed to stockholders, bankers, and other outsiders.

b To detect fraud on the part of company personnel.

c To assist the accounting department of the company in handling the heavy year-end work of preparing financial statements.

d To relieve management of the responsibility for financial reporting to stockholders and other outsiders.

___*c*___ **4** The primary objective of the internal auditor is to:

a Conduct an annual audit of a company's accounting system to determine that the financial statements present fairly its financial position and operating results.

b Observe the business transactions of the firm to be sure the annual tax returns are accurately prepared.

c Aid management by investigating and reporting on accounting, financial, and other operations of the company.

d Render a professional opinion as to the fairness and accuracy of the budget.

___*c*___ **5** Which of the following equations cannot be derived from the basic accounting equation (Assets = liabilities + owners' equity)?

a Assets − Liabilities = Owners' Equity.

b Liabilities = Assets − Owners' Equity.

c Owners' Equity = Liabilities − Assets.

d Assets − Owners' Equity = Liabilities.

___*a*___ **6** The balance sheet item, Retained Earnings:

a Appears in the stockholders' equity section for a corporation in which earnings have exceeded dividends.

b Is always equal to the amount of cash owned.

c Appears on the balance sheet of a single proprietorship if the earnings of the business have exceeded the withdrawals by the proprietor.

d Appears among the assets of any form of business organization in which earnings have exceeded amounts distributed to owners.

___*b*___ **7** Magic Forest Land Development Company sold a parcel of land at a profit. This will cause:

a A decrease in assets and liabilities.

b An increase in assets and owners' equity.

c An increase in assets and liabilities.

d A decrease in liabilities and owners' equity.

___*a*___ **8** Lake Arrowhead Boat Shop bought a $700 electric hoist to lift engines out of boats. The boat shop paid $200 in cash for the hoist and signed a note to pay the balance in 60 days. This transaction will cause:

a The boat shop's assets to increase by $700 and liabilities to increase by $500.

b Assets to increase by $500 and owners' equity to decrease.

c No change in total assets, but a $500 increase in liabilities and a similar decrease in owners' equity.

d No change in owners' equity, but a $500 increase in both assets and liabilities.

Exercises

1 In the space provided below, prepare a balance sheet for the Titan Corporation at December 31, 19__ from the following alphabetical list of accounts.

Accounts payable.........................	$ 28,000
Accounts receivable.....................	37,000
Automobiles............................	8,000
Buildings..............................	60,000
Capital stock..........................	100,000
Cash..................................	14,000
Income taxes payable...................	12,000
Land.................................	35,000
Office equipment.......................	16,000
Retained earnings......................	30,000

TITAN CORPORATION
Balance Sheet
December 31, 19___

Assets	$	Liabilities & Stockholders' Equity	
Cash	$ 14,000	Liabilities:	
Accounts Receiveable	37,000	Accounts Payable	$ 28,000
Buildings	60,000	In Tax Pay	12,000
Automobiles	8,000	Liab.	40,000
Land	38,000		
Office Equipment	16,000	Cap i	100,000
		R E	30,000
	$170,000		$170,000

2 Use the following information to complete the balance sheet of the Unitrex Corporation on December 31, 19___.

a The corporation was organized on January 1, 19___, and has operated for the full year 19___.

b Earnings have amounted to $100,000, and dividends of $20,000 have been paid to stockholders.

c Cash and Accounts Receivable together amount to three times as much as Accounts Payable.

UNITREX CORPORATION
Balance Sheet

Assets		Liabilities & Stockholders' Equity		
Cash	$ 42,000	Liabilities:		
Accounts receivable	144,000	Notes payable		$10,000
Land	90,000	Accounts payable		62,000
Building	260,000	Income taxes payable		40,000
Office equipment	56,000	Total liabilities		$112,000
		Stockholders' equity:		
		Capital stock	$	400,000
		Retained earnings		80,000
	$592,000			$592,000

TWO

RECORDING CHANGES IN FINANCIAL POSITION

HIGHLIGHTS OF THE CHAPTER

1 Many businesses engage in hundreds or even thousands of business transactions every day. Obviously, it would be too costly and time-consuming to prepare a new balance sheet after each transaction. Instead, the effects of these transactions are stored in the *ledger* until the end of a month or year, when new financial statements are prepared.

2 A *ledger account* is maintained for every item on the balance sheet. Thus, we have a ledger account for each type of asset (such as Cash), for each type of liability (such as Accounts Payable), and for each element of owners' equity.

3 Each ledger account occupies a separate page in a loose-leaf book called a *ledger.* The ledger is a permanent, important, and basic accounting record. For example, the first page in a ledger might be the ledger account entitled *Cash.* It would show increases and decreases in cash, resulting from the many transactions in which cash is received or paid.

4 A balance sheet is usually prepared at the end of each month by listing the cumulative balances of accounts contained in the ledger.

5 A ledger page is divided into two sections by a vertical line drawn down the center of the page. The left half of the page is called the *debit* side; the right half of the page is the *credit* side.

6 An amount recorded on the left side of a ledger page is called a *debit entry;* an amount recorded on the right side is called a *credit entry.*

7 Asset accounts normally have debit balances; that is, the amounts entered on the debit (or left) side are larger than the amounts entered on the credit (or right) side. For example, Cash is an asset account and has a debit balance.

8 Liability accounts and owners' equity accounts normally have credit balances because the amounts entered on the credit (right-hand) side of such accounts are greater than the amounts entered on the debit (left-hand) side.

9 For all *asset* accounts, increases are recorded by debits, and decreases are recorded by credits.

10 For all *liability* accounts and *owners' equity* accounts, increases are recorded by credits, and decreases are recorded by debits.

11 The double-entry system of accounting (which is almost universally used) requires that equal debits and credits be recorded for *every* transaction.

12 Since every transaction results in recording equal dollar amounts of debits and credits (double entry), it follows that the total of the debit entries in the ledger must equal the total of the credit entries. It also follows that the total of the debit balance accounts must equal the total of the credit balance accounts. When this equality of debits and credits exists, we say the ledger is *in balance.* Otherwise, one or more errors must have been made in recording transactions.

13 Accounts are arranged in the ledger in the same sequence as they appear on the balance sheet: asset accounts first, then liabilities, and finally owners' equity. Each account has a number, but many numbers are skipped, so that later a new account may be inserted in the ledger if the business acquires a new type of asset, liability, or owners' equity.

14 A very small business could record transactions directly in the ledger as they occurred. However, this procedure would be inefficient and it would be difficult to locate errors because you could not locate all the parts of one transaction. Therefore, virtually every business also maintains a *journal,* or *book of original entry.* A journal is a chronological record listing the transactions in the order they occur.

15 The journal shows all information about one transaction in one place. It shows (a) the date of the transaction, (b) the account(s) debited, (c) the account(s) credited, and (d) a written explanation of the transaction.

16 After a transaction has first been recorded in the journal, each debit and credit is later transferred to the proper ledger accounts. This transfer is called *posting.*

17 At month-end, when all entries in the journal have been posted to the ledger, the debit or credit balance of each account is computed (unless running-balance-form ledger accounts are maintained). These balances are listed in a *trial balance.* The trial balance is a two-column schedule listing the names and balances of all accounts in the order they appear in the ledger. Debit balances are listed in the left-hand column of the trial balance, and credit balances are listed in the right-hand column. Since the total of the debit balances should equal the total of the credit balances, the totals of the two columns of the trial balance *should be equal,* if the ledger is in balance.

18 The trial balance proves that an equal number of debits and credits were posted to the ledger, and also that the arithmetic in determining the account balances was correct. However, it does not prove that all transactions were correctly recorded in the journal. For example, the trial balance would not disclose the omission of an entire transaction (both the debit and credit parts) from the journal. Also if the *right amount* of debits or credits were entered in the ledger but the entry was made to the *wrong account,* the trial balance would not reveal the error.

19 The trial balance is not a formal financial statement, but merely a preliminary step to preparing financial statements.

20 The balance sheet is prepared from the trial balance.

21 Businesses using computers maintain accounting records on magnetic tape instead of loose-leaf books (ledgers), but the accounting principles of analyzing and recording transactions and preparing financial statements *are the same* as for a manual system. An understanding of accounting concepts is more easily acquired by studying a manual system.

TEST YOURSELF ON RECORDING CHANGES IN FINANCIAL POSITION

True or False

For each of the following statements, circle the T or the F to indicate whether the statement is true or false.

 1 In a prosperous and solvent business the accounts with credit balances will normally exceed in total dollar amount the accounts with debit balances.

 2 The term *debit* may signify either an increase or a decrease; the same is true of the term *credit.*

 3 All transactions are recorded in the ledger accounts by equal amounts of debits and credits.

 4 A business transaction is always recorded in the ledger by entries to two or more different ledger accounts.

 5 An entry on the left side of a ledger account is called a debit entry, and an entry on the right side is called a credit entry, regardless of whether the account represents an asset, a liability, or owners' equity.

 6 Accounts representing items which appear on the left-hand side of the balance sheet usually have credit balances.

 7 Decreases in a ledger account are recorded by debits and increases are recorded by credits, regardless of whether the account represents an asset, a liability, or owners' equity.

 8 The balance of a T account is entered in small pencil figures opposite the last entry on the side having the larger column total.

 9 A trial balance with equal debit and credit totals proves that all transactions have been correctly journalized and posted to the proper ledger accounts.

 10 The sequence of the account titles in a trial balance depends upon the size of the account balances.

 11 A journal entry may include debits to more than one account and credits to more than one account, but the total of the debits must always equal the total of the credits.

 12 One advantage of using a journal and a ledger rather than recording transactions directly in the ledger accounts is that the journal provides all information about a particular transaction in one place.

 13 The purchase of a typewriter on account would be recorded as a debit to Accounts Payable and a credit to Office Equipment.

 14 Of the following eleven accounts, six normally have debit balances and five have credit balances: Accounts Receivable, Accounts Payable, Buildings, Capital Stock, Cash, Land, Machinery, Mortgage Payable, Notes Payable, Notes Receivable, Retained Earnings.

 15 A transposition error means a posting of a journal entry to the wrong ledger account.

T **F** **16** The footings, or memoranda totals of the entries in a ledger account, do not relate to a specific transaction, but are merely a step in determining the balance of the account.

T **F** **17** If a business transaction is recorded correctly, it cannot possibly upset the equality of debits and credits in the ledger.

T **F** **18** More knowledge of accounting is required to post amounts from the journal to the ledger than is required to record transactions in journal entry form.

T **F** **19** In a journal entry recording the purchase of a desk for $275.80, both the debit and credit were recorded and posted as $257.80. This *transposition error* would *not* be disclosed by the preparation of a trial balance.

T **F** **20** The double-entry accounting system means that transactions are recorded both in the journal and in the ledger.

Completion Statements

Fill in the necessary words to complete the following statements:

1 In accounting, the term *debit* refers to the _left_ side of a _worksheet led_, while the term *credit* refers to the _right_ side.

2 The unit of organization for a journal is the _Transaction_ and the unit of organization for the ledger is the _account_.

3 A T account is a simplified model of a formal ledger account and consists of only three elements: (a) an account _title_, (b) a _title debit_, and (c) a _credit_.

4 Increases in assets are recorded by _debit_ and decreases in assets are recorded by credits; increases in accounts appearing on the right side of a balance sheet are recorded by _credits_, while decreases in those accounts are recorded by _debits_.

5 Asset accounts appear on the _left_ side of the balance sheet and normally have _debit_ balances. Liability and owners' equity accounts appear on the _right_ side of a balance sheet and normally have _credit_ balances.

6 When a company borrows from a bank, two accounts immediately affected are _Cash_ and _Notes Payable_. The journal entry to record the transactions requires a _debit_ to the first account and a _credit_ to the second one.

7 If you charge a sweater at a clothing store where you have an account, the store will _debit_ _debit/credit_ your account for the amount of your purchase.

8 A journal entry shows (a) the _date_ of the transaction, (b) the _cash_ to be _paid_, (c) the _asset_ to be _received_, and also (d) an _account_ of the transaction.

9 When making a journal entry the _title LP_ column just to the left of the debit column is left blank. When the debits and credits are later _posted_ to the ledger, the _number_ of the ledger accounts are listed in this column to provide a convenient _coincidence_ with the ledger.

10 A _Trial Balance_ is prepared from the ledger accounts at the end of the month (or other accounting period) in order to prove that the total of accounts with _assets_ is equal to the total of accounts with _Liabilities_.

11 The journal may also be called the _____ _____ _____.

12 With respect to (a) posting, (b) journalizing, (c) preparation of a balance sheet, (d) preparation of a trial balance, and (e) occurrence of a business transaction, the normal sequence of these events is denoted by the following list of letters _____ _e b a d c_.

Multiple Choice

Choose the best answer for each of the following questions and enter the identifying letter in the space provided. _X a_

_d_ **1** Mohawk Corporation completed a transaction which caused both its total assets and its total liabilities to increase by $6,000. The transaction could have been:

a Purchase of a fork lift by paying $4,000 cash and issuance of a note payable for $6,000.

b Purchase of a drill press by a payment of $2,000 in cash and issuance of a $4,000 note payable.

c Sale of land costing $6,000 for $6,000 in cash.

d None of the above.

_____ **2** Red Hill Vineyards completes a transaction which causes an asset account to decrease. Which of the following related effects may also occur?

a An increase of an equal amount in a liability account.

b An increase of an equal amount in owners' equity.

c An increase of an equal amount in another asset account.

d None of the above.

_____ **3** The term *posting* means:

a Entering transactions in a book of original entry.

b Transferring debit and credit amounts from the journal to the ledger.

c Proving the equality of debits and credits in the ledger.

d Determining the balances of individual ledger accounts.

_____ **4** If a computer is acquired by paying $10,000 in cash and signing a note payable for $40,000:

a Total assets are increased and total owners' equity is increased.

b Total liabilities are increased and total owners' equity is decreased.

c Total assets are decreased and total liabilities are increased.

d Total assets are increased and total liabilities are increased.

_____ **5** Which of the following errors would *not* be disclosed by the trial balance:

a The collection of a $520 account receivable was journalized as a $520 debit to Cash and a $502 credit to Accounts Receivable.

b The collection of a $200 account receivable was journalized as a $200 debit to Cash and a $200 debit to Accounts Receivable.

c The collection of a $1,000 account receivable was journalized correctly, but the debit was posted to the Land account instead of Cash.

d None of the above.

_____ **6** The bookkeeper of the Midas Company made an error in posting from the journal to the ledger accounts. He posted a debit to Office Equipment as a debit to Accounts Receivable. The procedure which is most likely to disclose this error is:

a Refooting all the accounts in the ledger.

b Sending month-end bills to all customers.

c Taking a trial balance.

d Comparing the written explanation of the journal entry with the accounts mentioned in the journal.

_____ **7** If a trial balance is out of balance the most probable cause is:

a A transaction calling for a debit to an asset account and a credit to a liability account was entered in the journal as a debit to a liability account and a credit to an asset account.

b A transaction was entirely omitted from the records.

c An error was made in determining the balance of the Cash account.

d The balances of the Cash account and the Accounts Receivable account were switched in the preparation of the trial balance.

_____ **8** Parker Investment Company entered into a transaction which did not change total assets, total liabilities, or total owners' equity. The transaction could have been:

a The sale of land for cash at a price equal to the cost of the land.

b An investment of cash in the business by stockholders.

c The settlement of a liability by paying the creditor some asset other than cash.

d None of the above.

Exercises

1 A list of accounts used by Morrow Corporation and the rules for debiting and crediting accounts are given below. Analyze the following transactions and indicate which accounts should be debited and credited by placing the identifying number of the account in the appropriate column. After each number you enter in either column, place the letter identifying the rule which caused you to debit or credit that account.

Accounts

1 Cash
2 Accounts Receivable
3 Land
4 Building
5 Office Equipment
6 Notes Payable
7 Accounts Payable
8 Capital Stock

Rules of Debiting and Crediting Accounts

A Increases in assets are recorded by debits.

B Decreases in assets are recorded by credits.

C Increases in liabilities or owners' equity are recorded by credits.

D Decreases in liabilities or owners' equity are recorded by debits.

Transaction	Account(s) Debited	Account(s) Credited
Example: Purchased land, paying part cash and signing a note payable for the balance.	*3A*	*1B, 6C*
1 Purchased office equipment on credit.	5a	7C
2 Collected the amount owed by a customer.	1a	2B
3 Borrowed money from the bank, signing a 90-day note.	1a	6C
4 Sold a portion of the land at cost for cash.	1a	3B
5 Returned a portion of the office equipment purchased in **1** above. The supplier agreed to credit Morrow Corporation's account.	7D	5B
6 Paid the balance of the amount due on the office equipment.	7D	1B
7 Issued additional capital stock for cash.	1a	8C

2 Enter the following transactions of Sun Corporation in the T accounts provided; then prepare a trial balance at September 30, 19____.

(1) Issued capital stock of $70,000 par value for $70,000 cash.

(2) Borrowed $12,000 cash from a bank and signed a note payable for that amount.

(3) Purchased land and building for $90,000, paying $40,000 in cash and issuing a $50,000 note payable. The land was estimated to represent one-third of the total purchase price.

(4) Purchased office equipment on credit at a cost of $6,000.

(5) Added a balcony to a building at a cost of $5,000; agreed to pay contractor in full in 30 days.

(6) Returned part of the office equipment to the supplier and received full credit of $600.

(7) Made a partial payment of $3,000 on the amount owed for office equipment.

Cash

Sept 30 70,000	40,000
12,000	3,000

Notes Payable

	12000
	50,000

Land

30,000	

Accounts Payable

600	6000
3000	5,000

Building

60,000	
5,000	

Capital Stock

	70,000 Sept 8

Office Equipment

6,000	600
	~~3000~~

SUN CORPORATION
Trial Balance
September 30, 19____

	Debit	Credit
Cash...............	$ 39,000	$
Land................	30,000	
Building............	65,000	
Office Equipment.......	22,400	
Notes Payable..........		62,000
Accounts Payable........		17,400
Capital Stock...........		70,000
	$136,400	$132,400

THREE

MEASURING BUSINESS INCOME

HIGHLIGHTS OF THE CHAPTER

1 Two things can cause a change in the owners' equity in a business concern: (a) a change in the owners' investment (stockholders putting assets in or taking assets out of the business) and (b) profits or losses resulting from operation of the business.

2 The change in owners' equity resulting from profits or losses is very important to business concerns. Profits increase total assets and owners' equity. These profits may be either distributed to the stockholders as dividends, or retained in the business to help finance expansion and growth. Losses, however, reduce both total assets and owners' equity and make the business and its owners economically worse off.

3 The increase in owners' equity resulting from operating profitably is recorded in the balance sheet in the **Retained Earnings** account. Distributing profits to stockholders as **dividends** causes a decrease in total assets and owners' equity. This decrease in owners' equity decreases the Retained Earnings account. Thus, retained earnings represent only the profits **retained in the business.** Many large companies started with small investments, but were able to grow by operating profitably and reinvesting their profits in the business.

4 **Net income** is the term accountants use for the **increase in owners' equity resulting from profitable operation** of the business; **net loss** means the **decrease in owners' equity resulting from unprofitable operations.**

5 Net income (or loss) is measured by deducting the **expenses** of a given period from the **revenue** earned in that period. Thus, **revenue minus expenses equals net income.**

6 **Revenue is the price of goods sold and services rendered during a given period.** Revenue comes into existence when the goods are sold or the service is rendered, even though cash is not collected until some later date. If a customer buys our product on credit in July and pays us in August, we should recognize the revenue from the sale in July. In August we are merely converting one asset (an account receivable) into another asset (cash).

7 Revenue causes both assets (accounts receivable or cash) and owners' equity to increase. Sometimes revenue is defined as the inflow of cash and receivables from sales of goods and services during a period.

8 **Expenses are the cost of goods and services used up in the process of obtaining revenue.** Expenses are recorded when the good or service is used up, even though cash payment is not made until later. If we use electricity in January but do not pay the electric company until February, we should recognize the expense from using the service (electricity) in January. In February, we are merely paying a liability owed to the electric company.

9 Not all cash payments are expenses; for instance, cash used to buy a building is an exchange of assets, not an expense. **Expenses cause owners' equity to decrease.**

10 A **dividend** is a distribution of assets by a corporation to its stockholders. This causes owners' equity to change, but has **nothing to do with net income.** This kind of change in equity is a **change in the owners' investment** in the business. Dividends are dis-investments; they are **not expenses** of the business.

11 To be meaningful, net income must be measured **for some time period** (such as a month or year). To determine the net income of a time period, we must first measure the revenue and expenses of **that same time period.** The span of time for which net income is determined is called the **accounting period.**

12 Many transactions affect two or more accounting periods. A building, for instance, is an asset which is used up over 20 or 30 years. The cost of the building should be recognized as expense as it is used up, but that period of time is not precisely determinable in advance.

13 The rules of debit and credit for revenue and expenses are based on the changes caused in owners' equity. Revenue increases owners' equity; therefore revenue is recorded by a credit. Expenses decrease owners' equity; therefore expenses are recorded by debits.

14 Every transaction which affects a revenue or an expense account also affects a balance sheet account. For example, credits to revenue are usually offset by debits to asset accounts; debits to expense are offset by credits to asset or liability accounts.

15 A separate ledger account is maintained for each major category of revenue and expense. Revenue accounts have credit balances; examples are Fees Earned, Commissions Earned, and Sales. Expense accounts have debit balances; examples are Telephone Expense, Office Salaries, and Insurance Expense.

16 The sequence of accounts in the ledger is as follows: (a) assets, (b) liabilities, (c) owners' equity, (d) revenue, and (e) expenses. This sequence is called *financial statement order,* because the three groups of balance sheet accounts (assets, liabilities, owners' equity) come before the income statement accounts (revenue and expenses).

17 Buildings, office equipment, and other *plant assets* have limited useful lives over which the asset is used up. A portion of the cost of the asset becomes expense (price of goods used up) during each year of its use. This process of allocating the cost of a plant asset over its useful life ıs called *depreciation.* For example, if we acquire a $100,000 building with an estimated life of 25 years and no salvage value, the depreciation expense each year will be ⅟₂₅ of $100,000, or $4,000. To ignore depreciation would cause expenses to be understated and therefore net income would be overstated.

18 Depreciation differs from most expenses in that no immediate or near-term cash outlay is required. The cash outlay was made *in advance* when the plant asset was acquired.

19 The journal entry to record depreciation is made at the end of the period by a debit to *Depreciation Expense* and a credit to *Accumulated Depreciation.* The Accumulated Depreciation account, with a credit balance, appears on the balance sheet as a deduction from the related asset account. The net amount (asset cost minus accumulated depreciation) represents the undepreciated cost (benefits

remaining) of the asset. Undepreciated cost is also called *book value.*

20 No one sends us a bill to show us how much of our building was "used up" in a specific accounting period. The entry to record depreciation expense is based on our understanding of what constitutes "expenses." Entries to record expenses and revenue that are not evidenced by transactions in the current period are called *adjusting entries.*

21 After the adjusting entries, such as recognizing depreciation expense, are made, an *adjusted trial balance* is prepared to prove that the ledger is still in balance.

22 The *income statement* is a formal financial statement which lists the revenue, deducts the expenses, and shows the net income of a business for a specified period of time (the accounting period).

23 The income statement is of great interest to managers, investors, and other groups, but it has certain limitations. It is not entirely accurate, because many transactions overlap accounting periods and their effect on one period is merely an estimate. Also the economic significance of some events (such as the discovery of an oil well) cannot be objectively measured and reflected in the income statement.

24 The *statement of retained earnings* covers the same time period as the income statement. It shows the beginning balance of retained earnings, the net income or loss for the period, a deduction for any dividends, and the ending balance of retained earnings.

25 The *report form* of balance sheet contains the same information as the *account form* previously illustrated. However, in the report form the assets are listed and totaled in the upper half of the page. The liabilities and stockholders' equity constitute a separate section in the lower half of the page.

26 The stockholders' equity section of the balance sheet shows two items: Capital Stock, representing the amounts invested by stockholders, and Retained Earnings, representing the accumulated net earnings since the date of incorporation minus all dividends distributed to stockholders.

27 *Closing the accounts* means transferring the balances of the revenue and expense accounts at the end of each accounting period into an account used to measure net income, called the *Income Summary* account. If revenue (credit balances) exceeds expenses (debit balances), the Income Summary account will have a credit balance representing the net income for the period. If the expenses exceed the revenue, the Income Summary account will have a debit balance, representing a net loss. In either case, the Income Summary account is then closed by transferring its balance to the Retained Earnings account. Transferring a credit balance from the Income Summary (representing net income) causes the Retained Earnings account to increase; transferring a debit balance (net loss) into Retained Earnings causes that account to decrease.

28 The Dividends account is closed by transferring its debit balance to the Retained Earnings account. It does not go through the Income Summary because dividends are not an expense.

29 The principal purpose of closing the revenue and expense accounts is to reduce their balances to zero at the end of the period so that they are ready to measure the revenue and expenses of the next period.

30 Four journal entries are generally used to close the accounts: (a) close revenue accounts into the Income Summary, (b) close expense accounts into the Income Summary, (c) close the Income Summary into the Retained Earnings account, and (d) close the Dividends account into Retained Earnings. These journal entries are called *closing entries.*

31 After closing the accounts, an *after-closing trial balance* is prepared to prove that the ledger is still in balance. The after-closing trial balance will contain only balance sheet accounts since all others will have zero balances.

32 The accounting procedures covered thus far may be summarized in eight steps: (a) journalize transactions, (b) post to ledger accounts, (c) prepare a trial balance, (d) make end-of-period adjustments, (e) prepare an adjusted trial balance, (f) prepare financial statements, (g) journalize and post closing entries, and (h) prepare an after-closing balance.

33 We have defined revenue as the price of goods and services delivered or rendered to customers during a period and we have defined expenses as the price of goods and services used during a period, regardless of when cash payment is made. These definitions of revenue and expenses result in *accrual basis* accounting. An alternative to accrual basis accounting is *cash basis* accounting. Under cash basis accounting, revenue is not recorded until received in cash; expenses are recognized in the period in which cash payment is made. The cash basis does not give a fair measure of profitability. For instance, the cash basis ignores revenue earned but not yet received and expenses incurred but not yet paid. We shall therefore use only the *accrual basis* to determine net income.

TEST YOURSELF ON MEASURING BUSINESS INCOME

True or False

For each of the following satements, circle the T or the F to indicate whether the statement is true or false.

T F **1** If a real estate firm using the accrual basis of accounting sells a client's building in May but the commission is not collected until July, the revenue is earned in May and should be included in the May income statement.

T F **2** Expenses cause a decrease in owners' equity and are recorded by debits.

T F **3** If cash receipts are $10,000 greater than total expenses for a given period, the business will earn a net income of $10,000 or more.

T F **4** The journal entry to recognize a revenue or an expense must always affect an asset or liability account as well.

T **F** **5** Under accrual basis accounting, revenue is recognized when cash is received, and expenses are recognized when cash is paid.

T F **6** An expense may be recognized and recorded even though no cash outlay has been made.

T F **7** Buying a building for cash is just exchanging one asset for another and will not result in an expense even in future periods.

T F **8** Revenue increases owners' equity and is recorded by a credit.

T F **9** Revenue accounts are closed at the end of the period by debiting the revenue accounts and transferring their balances by crediting the Income Summary account.

T F **10** If a business is operating profitably, the entry to close the Income Summary account will consist of a debit to Income Summary and a credit to Retained Earnings.

T F **11** If expenses are larger than revenue, the Income Summary account will have a debit balance.

T **F** **12** The Dividends account is closed at the end of the period by transferring its balance to the Income Summary account.

T F **13** The entry to recognize depreciation is an example of an adjusting entry.

T F **14** An increase in an expense account is the equivalent of a decrease in owners' equity.

T F **15** An adjusted trial balance contains only balance sheet accounts.

T F **16** In a well-established business which had been audited annually by a CPA, it would be reasonable to expect the Depreciation Expense account and the Accumulated Depreciation account to have equal balances.

T F 17 Retained earnings represent an amount of cash available to pay dividends.

T F 18 The Retained Earnings account is closed at the end of each period, and begins the next period with a zero balance.

Completion Statements

Fill in the necessary words or amounts to complete the following statements:

1 Performance Products Company began business on July 7. The company made the following total cash sales: July, $18,000; August, $26,000. Sales on 30-day credit were July, $31,000 and August, $42,000. All the July credit sales were collected in August, and all accounts receivable originating in August were collected in September. The total revenue for July was $ ~~49,000~~ and total revenue for August was $ ~~68,000~~ . Total cash receipts in August were $ 57,000 .

2 A dividend is declared by the board of directors of Sonic Corporation on July 1, and is payable on August 10 to stockholders of record on July 31. The journal entry on July 1 would consist of a debit to _Dividends_ and a credit to _Dividends Payable_. The entry on August 10 would consist of a debit to _Dividends Payable_ and a credit to _Cash_ .

3 Owners' equity may be changed by either ~~added~~ losses _Stock_ and _profits_ or a change in the owners' _cash_ .

4 The Income Summary account is used to bring together the _R_ and _E_ _____ accounts.

5 The process of allocating the _Cost_ of a plant asset to expense as that asset is used up is called _Depreciation_.

6 Assets, liabilities, and owners' equity are the only accounts that will have balances after the _closing entries_ have all been completed.

7 If expenses exceed revenue, the Income Summary account will be closed into the _Ret._

Earnings account by an entry which Cred. _close_ the Income Summary account.

8 The principal distinction between expenses and dividends to stockholders is that expenses are incurred for the purpose of _making money_ . A similarity between the two is that both expenses and dividends cause a dec. _increase_ in _owners equity_ .

Multiple Choice

Choose the best answer for each of the following questions and enter the identifying letter in the space provided.

_C_ **1** On April 1, Hudson Company received and paid a $700 bill for advertising done in March. In addition to this bill, the company paid $6,100 during April for expenses incurred in that month. On May 2, Hudson Company paid a $4,600 payroll to employees for work done in April. Based on these facts, total expenses for the month of April were:

a $ 6,100
b $ 6,800
c $10,700
d $11,400

_a_ **2** If a journal entry recognizes revenue, the other part of the entry might:

a Increase an asset account.
b Increase a liability account.
c Decrease an asset account.
d Increase the Retained Earnings account.

_b_ **3** The principal difference between depreciation and most types of expense is that depreciation:

a Is deductible only in years in which a profit is earned.
b Does not require an immediate or near-term cash outlay.
c Can be avoided if management creates a cash fund for use in replacing worn-out assets.
d Is subject to more precise measurement.

_c_ **4** Of the following accounts, which one would *not* appear in an after-closing trial balance?

a Accumulated Depreciation.
b Accounts Receivable.
c Depreciation Expense.
d Retained Earnings.

_a_ **5** If a journal entry recognizes an expense, the other part of the entry might:

a Increase an asset account.
b Decrease the Retained Earnings account.

c Decrease a liability account.

d Increase a liability account.

_____ 6 The statement of retained earnings:

a Shows the revenue and expenses of a business for a given time period.

b Indicates whether the cash position of the corporation will permit the payment of dividends.

c Provides a link between the income statement and the balance sheet.

d Has no relationship with the balance sheet.

_____ 7 Dividends on capital stock:

a Are recorded by a debit to Dividends, and this account is later closed into Retained Earnings.

b Are shown on the income statement among general administrative expenses.

c Are recorded in the accounts by a debit to Dividends Payable and a credit to Retained Earnings.

d Are recorded by a debit to Income Summary and a credit to Dividends Paid.

_____ 8 Gulfside, Inc., had net income of $92,000 during the current year and paid dividends of $48,000. If the balance of the Retained Earnings account at the end of the year was $250,000, the beginning balance was:

a $294,000

b $206,000

c $390,000

d $110,000

Exercises

1 Using the adjusted trial balance below, prepare (a) an income statement, (b) a statement of retained earnings, and (c) a balance sheet in **report form** for Mission Auto Repair, Inc., for the month ended May 31, 19___. The company adjusts and closes its accounts each month. Use the partially filled-in forms on the bottom of this page.

MISSION AUTO REPAIR, INC.

Adjusted Trial Balance

May 31, 19___

	Debit	Credit
Cash.	$ 21,600	
Notes receivable.	4,000	
Accounts receivable.	42,000	
Garage equipment.	33,600	
Accumulated depreciation: garage equipment.		$ 9,100
Notes payable.		8,200
Accounts payable.		10,300
Capital stock.		30,000
Retained earnings.		40,000
Dividends.	8,000	
Repair revenue.		27,000
Rent expense.	2,000	
Wages expense.	11,000	
Advertising expense.	1,400	
Utilities expense.	300	
Depreciation expense: office equipment.	700	
	$124,600	$124,600

a **MISSION AUTO REPAIR, INC.**

Income Statement

For the Month Ended May 31, 19___

Repair Revenue		27,000
Rent Ex	2000	
Wages Ex	11000	
Ad Ex	1400	
Util. Ex	300	
Depr. Ex	700	
Total	15400	15,400
Net Income		11,600

b **MISSION AUTO REPAIR, INC.**

Statement of Retained Earnings

For the Month Ended May 31, 19___

Retained Earn. (b)		40,000
Net In		11,600
Sub Tot.		51,600
Div.		8,000
Total R.E. End		93,600

c **MISSION AUTO REPAIR, INC.**

Balance Sheet

May 31, 19___

Assets		
Cash		21,600
Notes Rec.		4,000
Acc. Rec.		42,000
Garage Equip	33600	33,600
Acc dep Garage Equip	9,100	24,500
Total		92,100
Liabilities & Stockholders' Equity		
Notes Payable		8,200
Acc Payable		10,300
Total Liab.		18,500
Capital Stock	30,000	
R.E	43,600	73,600
Total		92,100

2 Indicate the effect of the following errors on each of the accounting elements described in the column headings below. Use the following symbols:

O = overstated, *U* = understated, *NE* = no effect

Error	Total Revenue	Total Expenses	Net Income	Total Assets	Total Liabilities	Total Owners' Equity
Example: Rendered services to a customer and received immediate payment in cash but made no record of transaction.	U	NE	U	U	NE	U
1 Payment for repairs erroneously debited to Building account.	NE	U	O	NE	NE	O
2 Recorded collection of an old account receivable by debiting Cash and crediting a revenue account.	O	NE	O	NE	NE	O
3 Failed to record depreciation for the current period.	Ne	U	O	O	U	NE
4 Recorded declaration of a dividend to be paid in a later month by debiting Dividends and crediting Retained Earnings.	O	U	NE	NE	U	O
5 Recorded the purchase of office equipment for cash as a debit to Office Equipment and a credit to Depreciation Expense.	NE	NE	O	O	NE	O
6 Recorded cash payment for advertising by debiting Repairs Expense and crediting Cash.	NE	NE	NE	NE	NE	NE

FOUR

COMPLETION OF THE ACCOUNTING CYCLE

HIGHLIGHTS OF THE CHAPTER

1 Many business transactions are begun in one accounting period and completed in a later period. A precise cutoff of transactions at the end of each accounting period is essential to the preparation of accurate financial statements.

2 *Adjusting entries* are made at the end of the accounting period to apportion transactions between periods. We want to be sure that the income statement contains all revenue earned and all expenses incurred in the period covered, but does not contain any revenue or expense applicable to the following period. Similarly, the balance sheet must contain all the assets owned and all liabilities owed on the last day of the period.

3 Every adjusting entry affects both a balance sheet account and an income statement account. Two purposes are accomplished by adjusting entries: (a) the proper amount of revenue and expense is apportioned to the current accounting period and (b) the proper amount of related asset or liability is established for the balance sheet.

4 Four types of transactions requiring adjusting entries are recorded costs, recorded revenue, unrecorded expenses, and unrecorded revenue. *Recorded costs* consist of costs which have been recorded in one period, but will benefit more than one accounting period. A fire insurance policy, for example, may cost $3,600 and run for three years. In this case, $\frac{1}{36}$ of the policy is used up in each month and should be recognized as an expense of that month. A recorded-cost adjusting entry at the end of each month would transfer to expense the portion of the total cost that had been used up in the period. In journal entry form, we would debit Insurance Expense $100 and credit Unexpired In-

surance $100. Depreciation is another recorded-cost adjusting entry.

5 *Recorded-revenue* adjusting entries are necessary when revenue has been received (and therefore recorded) before it has been earned. An example is a fee received in advance for services we are to render in the future. When we are paid in advance, a liability exists either to render the service or to refund the customer's money. As we render the service (or deliver the goods), we are earning the revenue and reducing our liability. At the end of the period, an adjusting entry would be made debiting (reducing) the liability and crediting a revenue account for the portion of the advance payments we have earned during the period.

6 *Unrecorded-expenses* adjusting entries are necessary when an expense has been incurred, but payment will not have to be made until a future period. For example, if employees will not be paid until February 2 for work they had done in January, the cost of this work should be recognized as expense in January. Also, at the end of January, a liability exists to pay the employees. The unrecorded-expense adjusting entry at the end of January would debit Wages Expense (to recognize the expense in January) and credit Wages Payable (to record the liability to make a future payment).

7 Revenue which has been earned but not yet recorded must be brought on the books by an *unrecorded-revenue* adjusting entry. For example, at the end of a period, services may have been rendered but no accounting entry made and no bill sent to the customer. The necessary adjusting entry would debit an account receivable and credit a revenue account.

8 Because so much detailed work is necessary at the end of the period in adjusting and closing the books and preparing financial statements, it is easy

to make errors. One way to simplify this work and avoid errors in the permanent accounting records is to use a **work sheet.**

9 A work sheet is a large columnar sheet of paper, prepared in pencil, and organizing all accounting data required at the end of the period. An error made on the work sheet is easily corrected; furthermore, it is self-balancing so that many types of errors are automatically brought to light. The work sheet is a working tool of the accountant which helps him prepare accurate financial statements at the end of the period. It also serves as a guide to making the necessary adjusting and closing entries in the accounting records. The work sheet, as the name suggests, is not a financial statement nor part of the permanent accounting records. It is the source from which financial statements are prepared, and from which adjusting and closing entries are made in the journal.

10 To prepare a work sheet, carry out the following steps:

a Enter ledger account balances in the Trial Balance columns.

b Enter all necessary adjusting entries in columns 3 and 4, the Adjustments columns.

c Combine the trial balance amounts with the related adjustments and enter the adjusted balances in the Adjusted Trial Balance columns.

d Extend the amounts in the Adjusted Trial Balance columns horizontally across the work sheet into one of the six remaining columns. Revenue and expense accounts go to the Income Statement columns. The amounts in the Retained Earnings account and the Dividends account go to the Retained Earnings columns. Assets, liabilities, and capital stock go to the Balance Sheet columns.

e Total the Income Statement columns and enter the net income or net loss as the balancing figure. This net income or net loss is also entered in the Retained Earnings columns.

f Compute the ending amount of retained earnings and enter this amount as a balancing figure in both the Retained Earnings columns and the Balance Sheet columns. Total both pairs of columns.

11 Financial statements are easily prepared from the work sheet as the data needed are already classified in the last six columns.

12 Adjusting entries are entered in the journal by taking data directly from the Adjustments columns of the work sheet. Preparation of closing entries from the work sheet may be summarized as follows:

a Close the revenue accounts by debiting each account listed in the credit column of the Income Statement columns, and credit Income Summary.

b Close the expense accounts by crediting each account in the debit column of the Income Statement columns, and debiting Income Summary.

c To close the Income Summary account, transfer the balancing figures of the Income Statement columns of the work sheet (also the balance of the Income Summary account) to the Retained Earnings account.

d Close the Dividends account by debiting the Retained Earnings account and crediting the Dividends account.

13 When a work sheet is used, the sequence of procedures making up the accounting cycle may be summarized in six steps:

a Record all transactions daily in the journal.

b Post journal entries to ledger accounts.

c Prepare the work sheet.

d Prepare financial statements from the work sheet.

e Enter adjusting and closing entries in the journal using the work sheet as a source. Post these entries to ledger accounts.

f Prepare an after-closing trial balance.

14 Most companies prepare **monthly** financial statements from work sheets, but close the accounts only once a year. Monthly and quarterly financial statements are called **interim statements.**

TEST YOURSELF ON COMPLETION OF THE ACCOUNTING CYCLE

True or False

For each of the following statements, circle the T or the F to indicate whether the statement is true or false.

T F 1 Companies which choose to close their accounts only once a year may nevertheless prepare monthly financial statements by use of work sheets.

T F 2 Adjusting entries are entered in the journal before the work sheet is prepared.

T *F* 3 If all transactions were originally recorded in conformity with general accepted accounting principles, there would be no need for adjusting entries at the end of the period.

T F 4 Adjusting entries contribute to accurate financial reporting by allocating revenue to the period in which it was earned and expenses to the period in which they were incurred.

T *F* **5** Every adjusting entry must change both an income statement account and a balance sheet account.

T **F** **6** An account entitled Unearned Rental Commissions is a liability account.

T **F** **7** The adjusting entry to allocate the cost of a three-year fire insurance policy to expense will cause total assets to increase.

T **F** **8** The adjusting entry to recognize that commission revenue not previously recorded (or billed to a customer) has now been earned will cause total assets to increase.

T **F** **9** The adjusting entry to recognize an expense which has not yet been recorded and will not be paid until some future period will cause total assets to decrease.

T **F** **10** The adjusting entry to recognize that a fee received in advance from a customer has now been earned will cause total liabilities to increase.

T **F** **11** If employees have worked eight days in a period for which they will not be paid until the first payday next period and if no adjusting entry is made at the end of this period, total liabilities will be understated and both net income and owners' equity will be overstated.

T **F** **12** The original cost of a building minus the accumulated depreciation is called the **book value,** or **carrying value.**

T **F** **13** The Balance Sheet credit column of the work sheet usually contains only liability accounts and owners' equity accounts.

T **F** **14** The balances of any unearned revenue accounts will appear in the Income Statement credit column of the work sheet.

T *F* **15** On a work sheet the figure representing net income for the period is entered in the Income Statement debit column and the Retained Earnings credit column.

T **F** **16** Sullivan's Car Wash borrowed $10,000 from its bank on June 1, signing a six-month, 9% interest-bearing note for that amount. The proper adjusting entry at June 30 will be a $75 debit to an expense account and a $75 credit to a liability account.

T **F** **17** A separate trial balance is unnecessary when a work sheet is used.

T **F** **18** The total of the Balance Sheet columns of the work sheet will usually be the same as the totals appearing on a formal balance sheet.

T **F** **19** The Adjustments columns of the work sheet for Martin's Cabinet Shop contained only two adjustments: one to allocate a portion of the three-year fire insurance

policy to expense, and the other to record the earning of a revenue which had been received in advance. The totals of the Adjusted Trial Balance columns would be larger than the totals of the Trial Balance columns.

T **F** **20** If a business operates unprofitably, the amount of the net loss will appear on the work sheet as a balancing figure in the Income Statement debit column and in the Retained Earnings credit column.

Completion Statements

Fill in the necessary words or amounts to complete the following statements:

1 The four types of transactions requiring adjusting entries are ___Unearned___ ___Revenues___ ___uneared___ ___Expenses___, ___Intrest___ ___on loans___, and ___Salaries___ ___Payable___ transactions.

2 An adjusting entry at November 30 concerning the cost of an insurance policy serves two purposes: (a) it ___credits___ the proper amount of ___Unexpired Insurence___ to November operations, and (b) it reduces the ___credit___ account entitled ___Insurence expense___ _____ so that the correct amount will appear on the November 30 balance sheet.

3 Adjusting entries always recognize either a ___asset___ _____ or an ___liability___.

4 The adjusting entry to record receiving some of the benefits in the current period from an expenditure made in an earlier period consists of a ___debit___ to an ___expense prepaid___ account and a ___credit___ to an ___pre exp.___ account.

5 If a customer pays in advance for services to be rendered, the entry to record the receipt of his payment consists of a ___debit___ to an ___cash___ account and a ___credit___ to a ___Unearned___ account.

6 If an expense has been accumulating from day to day (such as wages) without being recorded, the proper adjusting entry would ___debit___ an ~~tot~~ ___exp. Liab___ account and ___credit___ a ___expense___ account.

7 If an expenditure will yield benefits to a business only during the period in which it is made, the entry for the expenditure consists of a _debit_ to an _Revenie_ account and a _credit_ to an _Liab._ account and/or a _Exp._ account.

8 If an expenditure will yield benefits to the business of several periods, the entry for the expenditure consists of a _debit_ to an _asset_ account and a credit to an _Liabilitie_ account and/or a _Expense_ account.

9 In the work sheet prepared by a business operating at a loss, the Income Statement _debit_ column will exceed the _credit_ column and the excess of the _debit_ over the _credit_ will be entered in the _credit_ column in order to bring the two Income Statement columns into balance.

10 The South Bay Management Company agreed to manage an apartment building beginning May 15, 19___, for 1 year at a commission of $400 per month. The first $400 payment is received June 15, 19___. The adjusting entry at May 31, 19___, should consist of a debit to _Rev. Recieveable_ and a credit to _Unearned Revenue_. When the first payment is received on June 15, the collection should be recorded by an entry debiting _Unearned Rev_ for $400, and crediting _____ _____ for $ _____ and _____ _____ for $_____ .

Multiple Choice

Choose the best answer for each of the following questions and enter the identifying letter in the space provided.

___d___ **1** An adjusting entry should never consist of:
a A debit to an asset and a credit to revenue.
b A debit to an asset and a credit to a liability.
c A debit to expense and a credit to a liability.
d A debit to a liability and a credit to revenue.

___b___ **2** Assets would be overstated if a necessary adjusting entry were omitted for:
a Expired insurance.
b Accrued salaries.
c Accrued interest earned.
d Revenue collected in advance during the period.

___a___ **3** The preparation of a work sheet:
a Constitutes creation of a formal financial statement.
b Eliminates the need for entering adjusting entries in the journal.
c Provides the information needed for adjusting and closing entries.
d Serves no purpose unless the books are to be closed.

___a___ **4** The entry recording the liability to employees for work done during the period for which they have not yet been paid is an example of which type of adjusting entry?
a Recorded costs.
b Recorded revenue.
c Unrecorded expenses.
d Unrecorded revenue.

___b___ **5** Both the accounts for Depreciation Expense and Accumulated Depreciation:
a Are closed at the end of the period.
b Appear in the Trial Balance columns of the work sheet.
c Appear in the Adjusted Trial Balance columns of the work sheet.
d Appear in the after-closing trial balance.

___a___ **6** Failure to make an adjusting entry to recognize accrued interest receivable would cause:
a An understatement of assets, net income, and owners' equity.
b An understatement of liabilities and an overstatement of net income and owners' equity.
c An overstatement of assets, net income, and owners' equity.
d No effect on assets, liabilities, net income, and owners' equity.

___b___ **7** Which of the following adjusting entries will result in a decrease in assets and owners' equity?
a The entry to record the earned portion of rent received in advance.
b The entry to record accrued wages payable.
c The entry to record a revenue earned but not yet received.
d None of the above.

___d___ **8** A balance sheet account was debited in the amount of $1,240 for office supplies purchased during the first year of operations. At year-end, the office supplies on hand were counted and determined to represent a cost of $360. The appropriate adjusting entry would:
a Have no effect on net income.
b Consist of a debit to expense of $360 and a credit to the balance sheet account.

c Decrease assets $1,240.

d Increase expenses $880.

_b_ **9** Which of the following amounts appears in both the Income Statement credit column and the Retained Earnings debit column of a work sheet?

a Net income.

b Net loss.

c Accumulated depreciation.

d Dividends.

_c_ **10** When a work sheet is used, the normal sequence of accounting procedures would call for:

a Journalizing the adjusting entries before preparing the work sheet.

b Posting adjusting entries to the ledger after preparing an after-closing trial balance.

c Preparing a work sheet before journalizing adjusting and closing entries.

d Journalizing closing entries before preparing an adjusted trial balance.

Exercises

1 Use the adjustments below to complete the work sheet on page 22 for the month ended June 30, 19___ . (Corporate income taxes are to be ignored.)

a Unexpired insurance at June 30 amounted to $300.

b Office supplies on hand were determined by count to amount to $1,250.

c The office equipment is being depreciated on the basis of a 10-year life with no salvage value. Record one month's depreciation.

d Accrued interest on notes payable at June 30 amounted to $50.

e Commissions still unearned at June 30 amounted to $700.

f Accrued salaries payable at June 30 were $200.

	Trial Balance		Adjustments		Adjusted Trial Balance		Income Statement		Retained Earnings		Balance Sheet	
	Debit	Credit	Debit	Credit	Debit	Credit	Debit	Credit	Debit	Credit	Debit	Credit
Cash	4,800				4800						4800	
Accounts receivable	17,600				17600						17600	
Unexpired insurance	360			60	300						300	
Office supplies	1,900			650	1250						1250	
Office equipment	4,800				4800						4800	
Accumulated depreciation: office equipment		560		40		600						600
Notes payable		8,000				8000						8000
Accounts payable		1,800				1800						1800
Unearned commissions		1,500	800			700						700
Capital stock		9,000				9000						9000
Retained earnings, June 1, 19—		7,000				7,000				7600		
Dividends	1,000				1,000				1,000			
Commissions earned		16,000		800		16,800		16,800				
Rent expense	2,400				2,400		2,400					
Salaries expense	11,000		200		11,200		11,200					
	43,860	43,860										
Insurance expense			60		60		60					
Office supplies expense			650		650		650					
Depreciation expense: office equipment			40		40		40					
Interest expense			50		50		50					
Interest payable				50		50						50
Salaries payable				200		200						200
			1,800	1,800	44150	44150	14400	16,800				
Net income							2400			2400		
							16,800	16800	1000	9400		8400
Retained earnings, June 30, 19—									8400			
									9400	9400	28750	28750

2 On the journal page below, prepare adjusting and closing entries using the information contained in the work sheet prepared in Exercise 1.

General Journal

19___		Adjusting Entries		
		(a)		
June	30	Insurence Exp	300	
		Prepaid Ins.		30060
		(b)		
	30	Off. Sup. Exp	650	
		Off Sup.		650
		(c)		
	30	Dep Exp Off equip	40	
		& accum Dep. Off. Equip		40
		(d)		
	30	Intrest Exp	50	
		Intrest Pay		50
		(e)		
	30	Unearned Commis.	800	
		Commis. Earned		800
		(f)		
	30	Salaries Exp	200	
		Salaries Payable		200
		Closing Entries		
	30			
		Commissions Earned	16800	
		Income Summary		16800
	30	Income Summary	14,400	
		Rent Ex		2400
		Salaries Ex		11200
		Insurence Ex		60
		Office Suppl. ex		650
		Depr. exp. Off. Equip		40
		Intrest Ex		50
	30	Income Summary	2400	
		R.E.		2400
		R.E.	1000	
		Div.		1000

ACCOUNTING FOR A MERCHANDISING BUSINESS

FIVE

HIGHLIGHTS OF THE CHAPTER

1 A merchandising company is one whose principal activity is buying and selling merchandise. It uses the same accounting concepts and methods as the service-type business we studied in Chapters 1 to 4. The merchandising company, however, requires some other accounts and techniques to control and record the purchase and sale of merchandise.

2 The principal source of revenue for a merchandising concern is from the sale of goods. To succeed, it must sell its goods at prices higher than the prices paid in acquiring these goods from manufacturers or other suppliers. The selling price of goods in a retail store must cover both (a) the cost of the goods to the store and (b) the operating expenses such as rent and advertising, and still leave a reasonable profit (net income).

3 An income statement for a merchandising concern consists of three main sections: (a) the revenue section, (b) the *cost of goods sold* section, and (c) the operating expense section.

4 The *revenue* of a merchandising concern comes from *selling goods to customers.* A sale of merchandise is recorded by debiting Cash or Accounts Receivable and crediting a revenue account called *Sales.*

5 The *cost of goods sold* section of an income statement shows the cost of the merchandise sold during the period. This cost of goods sold is then subtracted from the sales revenue (the price for which the goods were sold). The *difference* between the sales revenue and the cost of the goods sold is called *gross profit.* Gross profit is the *excess* of the sales price of goods sold over the seller's cost for those goods. Gross profit may be stated as a *percentage of sales* which is called the *gross profit rate.*

6 An *inventory* of merchandise consists of the stock of goods on hand and available *for sale to customers.*

7 There are two alternative approaches to determining the amount of inventory and the cost of goods sold: (a) the *perpetual inventory system* and (b) the *periodic inventory system.*

8 For articles of high unit value, such as automobiles, the *perpetual inventory system* is appropriate. As each unit is sold, its cost is transferred from the Inventory account to an account called *Cost of Goods Sold.* Thus we have a perpetual or running record of the cost of goods sold during the period and the cost of goods on hand. In this chapter, however, we will concentrate on the *periodic inventory system,* which is very widely used.

9 The cost of goods sold section of the income statement for the month of May of a merchandising business using the *periodic inventory system* is shown below:

Cost of goods sold:	
Inventory (Apr. 30).....................	$ 5,100
Purchases..........................	6,300
Cost of goods available for sale	$11,400
Less: Inventory (May 31)...............	5,400
Cost of goods sold...................	$ 6,000

10 Under the periodic inventory system, the accounting records do not show from day to day the cost of the goods on hand (inventory) or the cost of goods sold during the period. Instead, the value of the inventory is determined *at the end of each accounting period* by taking a physical count of the merchandise on hand. The quantity of each item is then multiplied by an appropriate cost price, and the total value of the inventory is computed by adding the cost of the various items on hand.

11 The *cost of goods sold* is then computed by the following steps:

a Add the goods on hand at the beginning of the period (the inventory from last period) plus any additional goods acquired during the period (purchases) to get the *cost of goods available for sale.*

b From the cost of goods available for sale, subtract the goods which were not sold (namely, the inventory on hand at the end of the current period) to get the *cost of goods sold* during the period.

12 The cost of goods (*for resale to customers*) acquired during the period are recorded by debiting an account called *Purchases* and crediting Cash or Accounts Payable.

13 Several other factors may have to be considered in computing the cost of goods sold. For example, when merchandise purchased is found to be unsatisfactory and is returned to the supplier, the return is recorded by debiting Accounts Payable and crediting *Purchase Returns and Allowances.* Purchase Returns and Allowances must then be *deducted* from Purchases in the cost of goods sold section of the income statement because the cost of goods that were returned to the supplier should not be included in the cost of goods available for sale.

14 The freight charges on goods acquired during the period are a legitimate part of the cost of goods available for sale. Freight charges on *inbound* shipments of merchandise are recorded by debiting an account called *Transportation-in.* Transportation-in must then be added to Purchases to determine the total cost of goods acquired during the period. Note: Do not confuse Transportation-in with the freight expense on *outbound* shipments. Freight on outbound shipments is a selling expense, not part of the cost of goods being acquired.

15 Look at an expanded cost of goods sold section, including Purchase Returns and Allowances and Transportation-in, in your textbook.

16 Just as a merchandising business may return goods to a supplier (a purchase return), the customers of the merchandising concern may occasionally find that the goods they bought are unsatisfactory and return them to the store. This is called a *sales return.* Sales returns are recorded by debiting *Sales Returns and Allowances* and crediting either the customer's account or Cash. Sales Returns and Allowances are deducted from Sales on the income statement, to show a *net sales* figure.

17 Closing entries for a merchandising business include entries to (a) eliminate the beginning inventory, (b) record the ending inventory, and (c) close the accounts relating to the sales and purchases of merchandise.

18 The beginning inventory is cleared out of the Inventory account by a debit to Income Summary and a credit to Inventory. The ending inventory is recorded in the accounts by a debit to Inventory and a credit to Income Summary.

19 Purchases, Transportation-in, and Sales Returns and Allowances have *debit* balances and are closed in the same entry that closes the *expense* accounts. Purchase Returns and Allowances has a *credit* balance and is closed with the *revenue* accounts.

20 In a work sheet for a merchandising business, the ending inventory does not appear in the trial balance. It is written on a line below the trial balance and the adjustments. The amount of the ending inventory is placed in the Income Statement credit column and in the Balance Sheet debit column. This treatment results in reporting the inventory on the income statement (in the cost of goods sold) section, and on the balance sheet among the assets.

21 Standard *classifications* are used on financial statements to make them easier to read and more informative. Standard classifications also help the banker and investor in making comparisons between companies.

22 On the balance sheet, assets are usually classified into three groups: current assets, plant and equipment, and other assets. *Current assets* consist of cash and items capable of being *converted into cash* within a short period without interfering with normal business operations. Examples are marketable securities, receivables, inventories, and short-term prepayments.

23 Liabilities are divided between current and long-term. Those debts which must be paid within one year or the *operating cycle* (whichever is longer) are called current liabilities. Those maturing at more distant dates are long-term. Accounts payable and accrued wages payable are examples of current liabilities.

24 The operating cycle is the period of time a business usually takes to perform its function of buying (or making) inventory, selling that inventory, and collecting the accounts receivable generated by those sales. This may be described as the period of time a business takes to convert cash into inventory, into accounts receivable, and then back into cash, as illustrated by the following diagram of the operating cycle:

(buy inventory) (sell inventory)   (collect receivables)

Cash → Inventory → Accounts Receivable → Cash

25 Current assets and liabilities are used to measure a firm's *solvency,* or debt-paying ability. One measure of solvency is the *current ratio.* The current ratio is computed by dividing the total of current assets by total current liabilities. A current ratio of about 2 to 1 is generally considered indicative of reasonable debt-paying ability.

26 Another measure of solvency is the amount of **working capital.** Working capital is the **excess** of current assets over current liabilities (current assets **minus** current liabilities).

27 In the income statement the concept of classification includes separating operating expenses from the cost of goods sold. Operating expenses are usually subdivided between selling expenses and general and administrative expenses.

TEST YOURSELF ON ACCOUNTING FOR A MERCHANDISING BUSINESS

True or False

For each of the following statements, circle the T or the F to indicate whether the statement is true or false.

T F **1** The accounting concepts and methods presented in Chapters 1 to 4 for a service-type business are not applicable to a merchandising business.

T F **2** The income statement of a merchandising business includes a separate section entitled Cost of Goods Sold. This feature is not found in the income statement of a service-type business.

T F **3** Gross profit is the profit the business would have made if all of the goods available for sale had been sold during the period.

T F **4** If the gross profit rate is 40%, this means that the cost of goods sold is 60% of the sales price.

T F **5** When a cash sale is made by a merchandising business, the transaction is recorded by a debit to Cash and a credit to Sales, whether or not the sales price exceeded the cost of the goods sold.

T **F** **6** The purchase of either merchandise or office equipment by a merchandising company would be recorded as a debit to Purchases and a credit to either Cash or Accounts Payable.

T F **7** The perpetual inventory system will reflect from day to day the cost of goods sold so far during the period and the current balance of goods on hand.

T **F** **8** The perpetual inventory system is appropriate for businesses handling high-unit-cost goods, such as automobiles or fur coats but is not practical for stores handling a large quantity of low-priced items.

T F **9** When the periodic inventory system is used, the inventory account is debited when merchandise is purchased and credited when goods are sold.

T F **10** The entry to record payment of a purchase invoice within the discount period will include a debit to the Purchase Discounts account.

T F **11** The Transportation-in account contains the freight charges paid on inbound shipments of merchandise and is added to the Purchases account, a step toward finding the cost of goods available for sale.

T F **12** When a periodic inventory system is in use, the cost of goods sold section of the income statement contains two amounts for inventory: a beginning inventory which is added in arriving at the cost of goods available for sale, and an ending inventory which is subtracted to determine the cost of goods sold.

T F **13** At the end of the period, the beginning inventory is eliminated by debiting Income Summary and crediting Inventory.

T **F** **14** If an error causes ending inventory to be overstated, net income will also be overstated.

T F **15** The beginning inventory figure on this period's income statement was the ending inventory figure on last period's income statement.

T **F** **16** The entry to place the ending inventory on the books consists of a debit to Inventory and a credit to Accounts Payable.

T **F** **17** In the work sheet the ending inventory amount will appear in the Income Statement credit column and the Balance Sheet debit column but will not appear in the Trial Balance columns.

T **F** **18** The operating cycle of a business is the period of time between payroll dates.

T **F** **19** A good system of internal control would require that the same person (or same department) be responsible for both the purchasing and the receiving of merchandise.

T **F** **20** The current ratio is used to measure the relative profitability of two or more companies.

T F **21** Short-term prepayments are part of a firm's working capital.

Completion Statements

Fill in the necessary words or amounts to complete the following statements:

1 If the operations of a company are so organized that one person or one department handles all aspects of a transaction from beginning to end, the system of _internal control_ is unsatisfactory.

2 Adding net purchases to the beginning inventory gives the _cost of goods available for sale_. Subtracting _ending inventory_ from this figure leaves the _cost of Goods Sold_.

3 The return of merchandise to Cougar Company by a customer would be recorded on Cougar Company's books as a debit to _Purchases Returns and Allowances_ and a credit to either _Cash_ or _Accounts Recievable_.

4 Glass Maker sells merchandise to Kay, Inc., for $2,000, terms 2/10, n/30. Kay, Inc., makes payment one week after the date of invoice by sending a check for $_1960_. The entry to be made by Glass Maker upon receipt of the check would consist of a debit to cash for $_1960_, a _debit_ to _Purchase Discounts_ for $_40_, and a credit to _Sales_ for $_2000_.

5 No continuous record of the cost of merchandise on hand is maintained under the _periodic inventory_ system. The ~~Asset~~ _Purchase_ account is _____ to record the acquisition of merchandise for resale to customers.

6 Under the periodic inventory system, the journal entry to eliminate beginning inventory involves a _credit_ to the Inventory account and a _debit_ to the _Income Summary_ account. The entry to enter ending inventory involves a debit to the _inventory_ account and a credit to the _Income Summary_ account.

7 Sales discounts cause a reduction in the amount received by the selling company and are therefore located in its income statement as _an a_ _____ _____. Purchase discounts reduce the amount paid by a company buying merchandise and are therefore shown in its income statement as ___ _____ _____ _____.

8 In a balance sheet employing the usual classifications, the three groups of assets would be _short term assets_, _____ ____ _____, and _____ _____. The two groups of liabilities would be _sh._ _____ _____ and _____ _____.

9 The period of time a business usually takes to convert cash into inventory, then into receivables, and finally back into cash, is called the _____ _____.

10 The amount by which current assets exceed current liabilities is called _____ _____. Current assets divided by current liabilities is called the _workable capital._ These two computations are made to measure the _____ of a business enterprise.

Multiple Choice

Choose the best answer for each of the following questions and enter the identifying letter in the space provided.

_b_ **1** Which of the following list of accounts is used to compute the cost of goods sold?

a Purchases, Inventory, and Sales Returns and Allowances.

b Gross Profit, Purchase Returns and Allowances, and Transportation-in.

c Inventory, Net Sales, and Purchases.

d None of the above.

_b_ **2** By adding the purchases during the period to the beginning inventory and deducting the ending inventory, we obtain an amount called the:

a Cost of goods available for sale.

b Cost of goods sold.

c Gross profit on sales.

d Operating expenses.

_d_ __ **3** The beginning inventory is removed from the books by a closing entry which:

a Debits Inventory and credits Income Summary.
b Debits Income Summary and credits Inventory.
c Debits Inventory and credits Cost of Goods Sold.
d Debits Cost of Goods Sold and credits Inventory.

__ **4** When a physical inventory is taken at the end of the year the entry to record the amount established by the count is usually combined with:

a An entry closing the Sales account and the Purchase Returns and Allowances account.
b An entry closing the Purchases account and the Transportation-in account.
c An entry closing the Dividends account.
d An entry closing the Income Summary account.

__ **5** The net sales of Bar Corporation were $200,000 for the current year. If the cost of goods available for sale was $180,000 and the gross profit rate was 35%, the ending inventory must have been:

a $70,000
b $130,000
c $50,000
d $63,000

__ **6** Which of the following measures would be most effective in creating a strong system of internal control in a merchandising business?

a Require two signatures of responsible officials on all purchase orders, receiving reports, and sales invoices.
b Delegate to an appropriate employee or supervisor full responsibility for all aspects of transactions with a designated group of customers or suppliers.
c Arrange for an annual audit by a firm of certified public accountants.
d Establish an organization structure that will provide

separate departments for such functions as purchasing, receiving, selling, accounting, and credit and collection, so that the work of one organizational unit tends to verify that of another.

__ **7** Amounts debited to Transportation-in should include:

a Freight costs on inbound shipments of merchandise only.
b Freight costs on all inbound shipments of assets.
c Freight costs on all inbound and outbound shipments of merchandise.
d All freight costs incurred by the business.

__ **8** The average time period between the purchase of merchandise and the conversion of this merchandise back into cash is called the:

a Accounting period.
b Fiscal year.
c Inventory distillation.
d Operating cycle.

__ **9** The Toy Castle, a retail toy store, had current assets of $72,000 and a current ratio of 2 to 1. The amount of working capital must have been:

a $144,000
b $108,000
c $72,000
d $36,000

__ **10** The inventory of January 1, Year 1, will appear in the financial statements prepared on December 31, Year 1, as:

a A deduction from cost of goods available for sale to determine the cost of goods sold.
b A deduction from purchases to arrive at net purchases.
c A current asset.
d None of the above.

Exercises

1 Show the effect of each of the following errors on ending inventory, cost of goods sold, gross profit on sales, and net income by placing the appropriate symbol in each column. (Assume periodic inventory system.)

O = overstated   **U** = understated   **NE** = no effect

	Ending Inventory	Cost of Goods Sold	Gross Profit on Sales	Net Income
a Ending inventory is understated.	U	O	O	NE
b Beginning inventory is overstated.	O	U		
c Purchases are overstated.	O NE	O	O	O
d Purchase returns and allowances are overstated.	NF			
e Transportation-in is understated.	NE			
f Ending inventory is overstated.	S	U		
g Beginning inventory is understated.	U	U		
h Net sales are understated.				

2 Insert the missing figures in the following income statement. Gross profit is 40% of net sales and net income is 10% of net sales.

Sales.			$ *161,000*
Sales returns & allowances.	$ 4,500		
Sales discounts.	1,500	*6,000*	
Net sales.			$ *155,000*
Cost of goods sold:			
Inventory, Jan. 1.		$ 22,000	
Purchases.	$ 98,500		
Transportation-in.	3,600		
Delivered cost of purchases.		$ *102,100*	
Purchase returns and allowances.	$3,100		
Purchase discounts.	2,000	*5,100*	
Net purchases.		*97,000*	
Cost of goods available for sale.		$ *119,000*	
Inventory, Dec. 31.		26,000	
Cost of goods sold.			*93,000*
Gross profit on sales.			$ 62,000
Operating expenses.			*50,500*
Net income.			$ *11,500*

$$\frac{62000}{x} \quad \frac{40}{100}$$

$$40x = 62$$

$$\overline{155,000} \quad \frac{40}{100}$$

SIX

ACCOUNTING SYSTEMS MANUAL AND EDP

HIGHLIGHTS OF THE CHAPTER

1 In the preceding chapters we have used the general journal entry as a tool for analyzing the effects of various financial transactions upon business entities. Although the general journal entry is an effective analytical tool, it is not the fastest way to record a large number of transactions. Every general journal entry requires writing at least two account titles and an explanation of the transaction, as well as posting at least two amounts to the ledger. Since many businesses engage in thousands of individual transactions every day, it is often necessary to streamline the recording process to save time and labor.

2 A **manual data processing system** is a means of providing increased speed and economy in the accounting process without using costly business machines or computers. This type of system **groups transactions** into like classes and uses a **special journal** for each class. This permits division of labor and specialization because each special journal can be maintained by a different employee. Time is also saved because special journals are designed to handle transactions with much less writing and posting than is necessary in the general journal.

3 About 80 or 90% of all transactions fall into four types. These four types and the corresponding special journals are:

Types of Transaction	Name of Special Journal
Sales of merchandise **on credit**	Sales journal
Purchases of merchandise **on credit**	Purchases journal
Receipts of cash	Cash receipts journal
Payments of cash	Cash payments journal

Any transaction not falling into one of the above four types will be recorded in the **general journal.**

4 The **sales journal** is used to record all transactions which are a debit to Accounts Receivable and a credit to Sales (sales on credit). Columns are provided for the date, customer's name, invoice number, and amount of sale. At the end of the month the amount column is totaled and the **total** posted as a debit to Accounts Receivable and a credit to Sales. Detailed postings are made throughout the month to accounts of individual customers in the **accounts receivable subsidiary ledger.**

5 In prior chapters we have assumed that all sales on credit to customers were posted as debits to a single account called Accounts Receivable. Now, with our revised assumption of large volume (perhaps hundreds of customers), we divide the ledger into three separate ledgers: (a) an **accounts receivable subsidiary ledger** with a page for each customer; (b) an **accounts payable subsidiary ledger** with a page for each creditor; and (c) a **general ledger** containing all accounts except those with individual customers and creditors.

6 When the accounts with individual customers are placed in a separate ledger, a single account with the title of Accounts Receivable continues to be maintained in the general ledger. This **controlling account** represents the **sum** of all the customers' accounts in the subsidiary ledger. A controlling account called Accounts Payable is also maintained in the general ledger representing all the accounts with creditors which form the accounts payable subsidiary ledger. The general ledger still is in balance since all the individual receivable and payable accounts are represented by these two controlling accounts.

7 The *purchases journal* is used to record all purchases of merchandise *on credit.* At the end of the month the journal is totaled and the total is posted to the general ledger as a debit to Purchases and a credit to Accounts Payable. During the month individual postings are made on a current basis to accounts with individual creditors in the *accounts payable subsidiary ledger.*

8 The *cash receipts journal* is used to record *all transactions involving the receipt of cash.* Separate columns are established for cash and for other accounts frequently debited or credited in this type of transaction, such as Sales Discounts and Accounts Receivable. Debit and credit columns are provided for Other Accounts; in these we write in the name of any other account affected, and at the end of the month we make an individual posting to that account in the general ledger. The totals of the columns for Cash, Sales Discounts, Accounts Receivable, and Sales are posted to the general ledger at the end of the month.

9 The *cash payments journal* is used to record all transactions involving a cash payment. Separate columns are established for Cash and for accounts such as Purchase Discounts, Accounts Payable, and Purchases which are frequently affected by a cash payment. Debit and credit columns are also provided for Other Accounts so that any account title required may be written in. The posting of the cash payments journal parallels that described for the cash receipts journal in paragraph **8** above.

10 Most transactions will be recorded in the four special journals we have described. Any transactions which do not affect cash or the purchase or sale of merchandise on credit will be entered in the general journal. Double posting will be required if a general journal entry affects accounts receivable or accounts payable. For example, when a customer returns merchandise for credit to his account, we post the credit to the accounts receivable controlling account in the general ledger and also to the individual customer's account in the accounts receivable subsidiary ledger.

11 Accounts with customers and creditors in the subsidiary ledgers are usually of the three-column, running balance type. The right-hand column shows the new balance after each debit or credit entry. Many companies also prefer this form of account for the general ledger.

12 *Posting references* provide a cross reference between ledgers and journals. We use the following symbols: *S,* sales journal; *P,* purchases journal; *CR,* cash receipts journal; *CP,* cash payments journal; and *J,* general journal. The symbol is combined with a number, so that in looking at any debit or credit entry in any ledger, we can identify the journal from which it came and the page number of that journal. (For example, *S7* as a posting reference in the accounts receivable subsidiary ledger would tell us that the debit to a customer's account came from page 7 of the sales journal.)

13 To prove that all ledgers are in balance at the end of the period, a trial balance of the general ledger is prepared, and in addition a list of the balances in each subsidiary ledger is prepared to prove that the total agrees with the related controlling account.

14 Many variations in special journals are possible. For example, a special column can be added for any account which is frequently debited or credited. An additional special journal can be created for any type of transaction which occurs frequently, such as sales returns by credit customers of a retail store.

15 Some businesses keep a file of invoices and post directly from these to the ledger accounts rather than copying data from invoices into a sales journal or a purchases journal. This system is called *direct posting from invoices.* At the end of the month the file of invoices is totaled, and a general journal entry is used to post the total to the controlling account in the general ledger.

16 Although a manual system of processing accounting data, strictly defined, would call for handwritten records, such machines as cash registers, multi-copy forms, desk calculators, and other machines are used in many small businesses.

17 *Mechanical accounting systems* utilize electrically powered machines that produce a variety of accounting records and reports. Punched cards are used to record accounting data such as account titles and amounts. The information punched on the cards can be read and processed by machines to produce almost any kind of report or analysis desired.

18 *Electronic data processing systems* use computers and related machines called *peripheral equipment.* EDP offers the advantage of incredible speed in processing data, plus the creation of additional current information not previously available to management.

19 The *computer* performs the *processing function,* which includes the storage of information, arithmetic computation, and control. *Input devices* prepare and insert information into the computer. *Output devices* transfer information out of the computer to accountants or other users and may print hundreds of lines per minute. Collectively, these machines are called *hardware.* Other materials necessary to the operation of an EDP system, such as computer programs, punched cards, magnetic tapes, and personnel, are called **software.**

20 A significant characteristic of an EDP system is that the units of equipment are interconnected so that the processing of data is a continuous operation from the point of reading input to the printing of a final report.

21 The EDP system makes possible a high degree of accuracy, but errors are still possible. The input data may be in error or the computer program (a set of instructions for the computer) may contain errors. The use of a computer does not guarantee that the output is accurate or reliable.

22 A strong system of internal control is necessary to ensure the reliability of computer output. These internal controls should include **input controls** and **program controls.**

 a **Input controls** are the precautions taken to ensure that input data entered into the computer are correct. Two common input controls are the use of **control totals** and a **verifier key punch.**

 b **Program controls** (or processing controls) are error-detecting routines built into the computer program. An **item count** and a **limit** (or **reasonableness**) **test** are examples of program controls.

23 The most common applications of computers in accounting are to process large amounts of data in routine operations, such as posting accounts receivable or preparing payrolls. However, many businesses use computer-based **integrated information systems** which fill all the data processing needs of the entire business. CPAs also use computers to perform many auditing procedures in the audit of large corporations.

24 The small business which cannot afford to own or lease a computer can still gain its advantages either by sending data out to a **computer service center** for processing, or by **time-sharing.** Time-sharing refers to using a large central computer by means of a portable terminal which is both an input and output device. Through terminals, many businesses may use the same central computer.

TEST YOURSELF ON DATA PROCESSING SYSTEMS

True or False

For each of the following statements, circle the T or the F to indicate whether the statement is true or false.

T F **1** Sale on credit of old office equipment no longer needed in the business would be recorded in the sales journal.

T F **2** The total of the Accounts Payable column in the cash payments journal is posted at the end of the month as a debit to Accounts Payable and a credit to Cash.

T F **3** The purchase of office supplies on credit is recorded in the purchases journal.

T F **4** Purchases of merchandise on credit are recorded in the purchases journal.

T F **5** The Accounts Receivable column in the cash receipts journal is intended for credit entries.

T F **6** When a customer is permitted to return merchandise for credit to his account, the transaction is usually recorded in the general journal.

T F **7** The sale of merchandise for cash is recorded in the sales journal.

T F **8** The total of the Other Accounts column in the debit section of the cash receipts journal is not posted to the ledger.

T F **9** If a trial balance of the general ledger is in balance, this proves that each controlling account is in agreement with the related subsidiary ledger.

T F **10** A subsidiary ledger for accounts receivable is usually arranged in alphabetical order of customers' names.

T F **11** **Double posting** of a general journal entry crediting Accounts Receivable means posting the credit to the controlling account in the general ledger and to a customer's account in the subsidiary ledger.

T F **12** When special journals, controlling accounts, and subsidiary ledgers are used, no posting to any ledger is performed until the end of the month.

T F **13** In an EDP system the computer is described as **hardware;** the term **software** describes the input devices used to prepare and insert information into the computer and the output devices which transfer information out of the computer.

T F **14** Computers have proved to be of great importance to business in speeding up the processing of data and improving the accuracy of accounting information. However, computers are **not** useful to CPA firms in making annual audits of a business, because auditing requires that financial statements be verified by reference to ledgers, journals, and source documents.

T F **15** Computer output will always be correct unless the computer malfunctions.

T F **16** Third-generation computers can actually

think and can solve problems which were not anticipated when the computer program was prepared.

T F 17 One input control is to have the computer add up the dollar total of items being processed and compare this sum with a predetermined control total.

T F 18 A *limit test* is a program control which will detect if any of the input data are missing.

T F 19 Computers are used to post accounts receivable and prepare payrolls but not to maintain journals and ledgers and prepare financial statements.

T F 20 *Time-sharing* is an input control which prevents input data from being processed a second time.

T F 21 A *limit test* and an *item count* would both be appropriate program controls in the preparation of weekly paychecks by computer.

Completion Statements

Fill in the necessary words or amounts to complete the following statements:

1 Special journals have the advantage of saving much time in journalizing and _Posting_ .

2 When merchandise is purchased on credit, the transaction is recorded in the _Sales Purchase_ journal. If a portion of the merchandise is returned for credit to the supplier, the return is recorded in the _General_ journal, and the _credit debit_ side of the entry is double-posted.

3 The column total of the sales journal is posted at the end of the month as a _credit_ to _Sales account_ and as a _debit_ to _cash A/R_

4 Some companies do not use a sales journal but instead post directly from the _Sales invoice_ to the customers' accounts in the accounts receivable ledger. When this is done, the _invoices accounts_ are totaled and an entry is made in the _general_ journal debiting the Accounts Receivable _Controlling_ account and crediting Sales.

5 A set of instructions which directs the computer how to process data is called a _program_ .

6 Information recorded in machine-sensible form for input to a computer may be on _cards_

tape, paper tape programs or _magnetic tape_ .

7 The printer in an EDP system is an example of an _output hardware_ device, and the reader is an _input software_ device. Such devices, along with the computer itself, are referred to as _hardware_. Punched cards, tapes, and programs are examples of _software_.

8 The symbol (X) placed below a column total in the cash receipts journal or cash payments journal means the column total should _not be posted_ .

9 A business will usually benefit by establishing a special journal for any type of transaction that _may occur frequently_

10 The amount of an employee's salary was accidentally keypunched as $8,000 instead of $800. A verifier key-punch is not used. A computer preparing paychecks should detect this error because the total payroll will not agree with the _control total_, and a _limit test_ should prevent an $8,000 item from being processed.

11 Sharing a central computer with other businesses is called _time sharing_. Each business communicates with the computer by using a _program terminal_.

12 An information system which is designed to meet the needs of the entire business rather than a single department is an _Idp_ system.

Multiple Choice

Choose the best answer for each of the following questions and enter the identifying letter in the space provided.

_d_ **1** The total of a single-column purchases journal is posted at the end of the month:

a As a debit to Accounts Payable and a credit to Purchases.

b To the Purchases account, Cash account, and Sales account.

c To the Purchases account only.

d As a debit to Purchases and a credit to Accounts Payable.

_C a_ **2** The Rex Company records all transactions in a two-column general journal but is considering the installation of special journals. The number of sales on credit during January was 325 and the number of sales for cash was 275. Therefore:

a The use of a sales journal in January would have saved 324 postings to the Sales account.

b The use of a cash receipts journal would have reduced the number of postings to the Cash account, but would not have affected the number of postings to the Sales account.

c The total number of transactions recorded in the sales journal (if one had been used in January) would have been 600, but only two postings would have been necessary from that journal.

d If special journals were installed, the entry to close the Sales and Purchases accounts at the end of the period would be made in the sales journal and the purchases journal, respectively.

_____ **3** The purchases journal is a book of original entry used to record:

a Purchase of any asset on credit.

b Purchase of merchandise for cash or on credit.

c Purchase of merchandise on credit only.

d Purchases and purchase returns and allowances.

_____ **4** A major advantage of controlling accounts is that their use makes it possible:

a To reduce the number of accounts in the general ledger.

b To determine on a daily basis the total amount due from customers and total amount owing to creditors.

c To reduce the number of entries in subsidiary ledgers.

d To increase the number of columns in special journals.

_____ **5** When a general journal and four special journals are in use, the entries in the Cash account will come:

a From all of the books of original entry.

b From the four special journals.

c From only two of the four special journals.

d Principally at month-end from adjusting and closing entries.

_____ **6** The cash receipts journal is used:

a For transactions involving a debit to Cash and debits or credits to other balance sheet accounts.

b For all transactions involving the receipt of cash, regardless of the number of other accounts involved.

c For transactions involving not more than two accounts.

d For transactions involving the receipt of cash but not affecting subsidiary ledgers.

_____ **7** The processing operations performed by a computer include storage of information, arithmetic

manipulation of data, and control. The term *control* in this context means:

a Subdivision of duties to reduce the opportunity for fraud or accidental errors.

b The ability of the computer to guide itself through the processing operations utilizing detailed lists of instructions concerning the work to be done.

c The ability of the computer to recognize and reject any errors included in input data.

d The making of judgment decisions independently of prior instructions.

_____ **8** Posting of accounts receivable with individual customers is done by computer. Credit sales totaling $19,742 were made to 809 customers. A key-punch operator made a key-punching error and recorded a $35 sale to Roger Jones at $53. Two controls which could detect this error are:

a An item count and a limit test.

b A limit test and a control total.

c A control total and a verifier key-punch.

d A verifier key-punch and an item count.

Exercises

1 For each of the following transactions, indicate the journal which should be used by placing the appropriate symbol in the space provided.

S = sales journal, **P** = purchases journal, **CR** = cash receipts journal, **CP** = cash payments journal, **J** = general journal.

a Sold merchandise on credit.................	S
b Purchased merchandise for cash............	CP
c Purchased truck for cash for use in business..	CP
d Collected account receivable and allowed a cash discount..........................	CR
e Recorded depreciation for the period........	J
f Made entry to close the expense accounts at end of period...........................	J
g Accepted note receivable from customer in settlement of account receivable...........	J
h Paid employee salaries....................	CP
i Made entry to accrue salaries at end of year...	J
j Sold merchandise for cash.................	CR
k Purchased merchandise on credit...........	P
l Returned merchandise to supplier for credit...	J
m Purchased office equipment on credit........	J
n Allowed customer to return merchandise for credit...................................	J

2 For each of the following general ledger accounts indicate the source of debit and credit postings by entering a symbol representing the proper journal. Use the same code as in Exercise 1.

	Debit	Credit
a Purchases.	P, J CP	J
b Purchase Returns and Allowances.	J	J, CR
c Purchase Discounts.	J	CP
d Sales.	J & CR	S CRJ CR
e Sales Returns and Allowances.	CR J J	J
f Sales Discounts.	CR J	J
g Accounts Payable.	J CP P	P, J
h Accounts Receivable.	S CR J	J CRJ
i Cash.	CR J	CP
j Depreciation Expense.	J	

FORMS OF BUSINESS ORGANIZATION

SEVEN

HIGHLIGHTS OF THE CHAPTER

1 Three common forms of business organization found in the American economy are: the single proprietorship, the partnership, and the corporation.

2 In a single proprietorship, a *capital account* and a *drawing account* are maintained in the ledger to show the equity of the owner. The Capital account is credited with the amount invested by the owner and with the net income earned by the business. The Capital account is debited when losses are incurred. Withdrawals by the owner are debited to a Drawing account, which is transferred to the Capital account at the end of the accounting period.

The same procedures are followed for a partnership, except that separate capital and drawing accounts are maintained for each partner.

3 The income statement for a single proprietorship does not include any salary expense for the owner or any income tax expense. The income statement for a partnership shows the amount of net income allocated to each partner but does not report an income tax expense since a partnership, like a single proprietorship, is not a taxable entity.

4 The principal characteristics of the partnership form of organization are:
a Ease of formation.
b Limited life.
c Mutual agency.
d Unlimited liability.
e Co-ownership of partnership property and profits.

5 *Advantages of the partnership* form of organization are:
a It brings together sufficient capital to carry on a business.
b It combines special skills of the individual partners.
c It offers freedom and flexibility of action.
d It may, in certain instances, result in income tax advantages to the partners.

6 *Disadvantages of the partnership* form of organization are:
a A partnership may be terminated upon death or withdrawal of a partner.
b Each partner is personally responsible for all partnership debts.
c The partnership is bound by the acts of any partner as long as these acts are within the scope of normal operations.
d The partnership is less effective than a corporation for raising large amounts of capital.

7 Factors that partners might consider in arriving at an equitable plan to divide net income include:
a Amount of time each partner devotes to the business.
b Amount of capital invested by each partner.
c Other contribution by each partner to the success of the partnership.

8 A *statement of partners' capitals* shows the changes in the partners' capital accounts during a fiscal period. Additional investments made by a partner and his share of net income are added, and withdrawals and his share of any loss are deducted from his beginning capital balance in arriving at his ending capital balance.

9 If the partnership profit-sharing agreement provides for salaries and interest, these provisions are to be followed even though the net income for the year is less than the total of the salary and interest allowances. The excess of the salary and interest allowances over the amount of net income is charged to the partners in the agreed residual profit and loss ratio.

10 A corporation is an "artificial being" which is regarded as a legal entity, having a continuous existence apart from that of its owners. Ownership in a corporation is evidenced by transferable shares of stock, and the owners are called *stockholders* or *shareholders.*

11 The *advantages of the corporate form* of organization are:

a It makes possible the bringing together of large amounts of capital under single nagement.

b Stockholders have no persona bility for the debts of the corporation and can never lose more than the amount of their investment.

c The shares of stock in a corporation are readily transferable.

d A corporation continues in existence despite changes in ownership or management.

e Management and ownership are sharply separated, and the corporation is able to employ the best professional managers available.

12 Some ***disadvantages of the corporate form*** of organization are:

a A corporation must pay a high rate of taxation on its earnings.

b Corporations are subject to considerable regulation of their business, and publicly owned corporations must make extensive disclosure of their affairs.

c The separation of ownership and management (effective control of corporate affairs) may result in management practices which are not in the best interests of the stockholders.

13 Corporate stockholders have certain ***basic rights:***

a To vote for directors and certain corporate actions.

b To share in profits by receiving dividends.

c To share in the distribution of assets if the corporation is liquidated.

d To subscribe to additional shares of stock when the corporation decides to increase the amount of stock outstanding. (This right has been relinquished in some corporations.)

14 The board of directors declares dividends, appoints corporate officers, approves officers' salaries, and generally approves important contracts.

15 A corporation is organized by filing an application with the appropriate state agency. The application contains the ***articles of incorporation*** and the list of stockholders and directors. Costs of organizing a corporation are recorded in an Organization Costs account and are generally written off as expense over a five-year period.

16 Corporations may obtain funds by issuing capital stock, by borrowing money, and by retaining the resources generated from profitable operations. The stockholders' equity in a corporation consists of the capital invested by stockholders (paid-in capital), and the capital acquired through profitable operations (retained earnings). The term ***deficit*** indicates a negative amount of retained earnings resulting from unprofitable operations.

17 Capital stock may be issued with (a) par value, (b) no-par value with a stated value, or (c) neither par nor stated value. The par value of stock is the ***legal*** capital which may be regarded as a minimum cushion of capital existing for the protection of creditors and which cannot be distributed to stockholders in the form of dividends. Most issues of capital stock have a par value.

18 Capital stock is quite often issued for a sum greater than the par (or stated) value; the excess is generally credited to Paid-in Capital in Excess of Par (or Stated) Value. Capital stock is rarely issued for less than par (or stated) value. In most states it is illegal to do so.

19 When stock is issued for non-cash assets, the ***fair market value*** of the non-cash asset or the ***market value*** of the stock issued should be used as a basis for recording the transaction.

20 When a large amount of stock is to be issued, the corporation may utilize the services of an ***underwriter,*** who guarantees the issuing corporation a specific price for the stock.

21 When capital stock is sold on a subscription basis, the accounting entry consists of a debit to Subscriptions Receivable: Capital Stock and a credit to Capital Stock Subscribed. Collections are recorded by debiting Cash and crediting Subscriptions Receivable: Capital Stock. Upon full payment of the subscriptions, Capital Stock Subscribed is debited and Capital Stock is credited. The stock certificates are then delivered to the investors.

22 In order to appeal to a large number of investors, a corporation may issue more than one class of stock. When only one class of stock is issued, it is generally referred to as ***common stock;*** when two or more classes of stock are outstanding, they usually consist of ***common stock*** and various types of ***preferred stock.***

23 In case of liquidation, a holder of preferred stock will almost always be entitled to receive full payment for his equity before holders of common stock receive anything. Preferred stock is generally ***callable*** at the option of the corporation and does not have voting rights as long as dividends on the preferred stock are paid regularly.

24 A share of ***convertible preferred stock*** can be exchanged for an agreed number of shares of common stock. A holder of convertible preferred stock has greater assurance of receiving regular dividends while at the same time sharing in any increase in the value of the common stock.

25 Market price of a share of stock depends on (a) the level of current and projected earnings, (b) the dividend rate per share, (c) the financial condition of the company, and (d) the current state of the investment market. Once stock is issued, further stock transactions on the open market are between investors, and such transactions do not affect the issuing corporation. The corporation will, however, update its **stockholders' ledger** by transferring the shares changing hands from one stockholder to another.

26 A corporation is subject to income taxes which are computed as a percentage of taxable income. Taxes on income are recorded by a debit to Income Taxes and a credit to Income Taxes Payable.

TEST YOURSELF ON FORMS OF BUSINESS ORGANIZATION

True or False

For each of the following statements circle the T or the F to indicate whether the statement is true or false:

 T F 1 Accounting principles generally are equally applicable to single proprietorships, partnerships, and corporations; however, the major differences are found in the accounting for the owners' equity in each of these forms of business organization.

T F 2 An owner's drawing account is found in all forms of business organization.

 T F 3 The owner's equity for a single proprietorship is typically reported in a single account; in a corporation the owners' equity may be reported in three accounts: Capital Stock, Paid-in Capital in Excess of Par, and Retained Earnings.

 T F 4 One of the adjusting entries for a partnership is the transfer of balances in partners' drawing accounts to their capital accounts.

 T F 5 Ordinarily there is no need to prepare a work sheet for a single proprietorship or a partnership.

 T F 6 Some states deny the incorporation privilege to persons engaged in certain professions (such as law and public accounting), because the stock issued by a service-type corporation would be too risky for investors.

 T F 7 One of the major advantages of a partnership over a corporation is that it makes possible the bringing together of very large amounts of capital needed to carry on a business.

 T F 8 In the absence of a specific agreement, the law requires that partnership profits be divided equally among the partners.

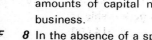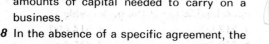 **T F 9** A reasonable profit-sharing agreement among partners would be one which takes into account the time that each partner devotes to the business, the amount of capital each invests, and other contributions of each partner to the success of the partnership.

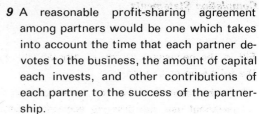 **T F 10** A partnership must file an income tax return even though it is not required to pay income taxes.

T F 11 The officers of a corporation cannot own stock in that corporation; they are professional managers and not investors.

T F 12 The expression "double taxation" refers to the fact that the net income of a corporation is taxed both by the state in which it is incorporated and by the federal government.

T F 13 Stockholders of a corporation elect the board of directors, which in turn appoints the top officers of the corporation.

T F 14 Frequently less than 10% of the stockholders attend the annual meeting of a large corporation.

T F 15 Cash dividends are declared by the board of directors, not by the stockholders of a corporation.

T F 16 The legal capital of a corporation consists of the par or stated value of all capital stock outstanding plus any paid-in capital in excess of par or stated value.

T F 17 A deficit will be reported in the balance sheet of a corporation if the cumulative net income is less than the losses plus the total dividends declared (if any) since the corporation was organized.

T F 18 Dividends on cumulative preferred stock are automatically declared but need not be paid currently; they are reported as a liability in the balance sheet.

T F 19 Common stock of Corporation X pays an annual $1 per share dividend and sells for $15 per share on the open market. The corporation's $1.80 convertible preferred stock is selling for $35 per share and is convertible into two shares of common stock. The holder of 100 shares of the convertible preferred stock should exchange his holdings for 200 shares of common stock because this action will increase his annual dividend revenue from $180 to $200.

T F 20 An underwriter guarantees the issuing corporation a set price for a new issue of stock and then resells the stock to the investing public at a higher price.

Completion Statements

Fill in the necessary words or amounts to complete the following statements:

1 If the owner withdraws merchandise for his personal use, his drawing account is debited for the _amount_ of the merchandise withdrawn.

2 Income tax expense appears in the income statement of a _corp_ but does not appear in the income statement of a _proprietorship_ _____ or a _partnership_.

3 A closing entry showing a debit to Income Summary for $20,000 and credits to the capital accounts of Allen and Baker for $15,000 and $5,000, respectively, indicates that the partnership reported a profit of $_20,000_ for the period and that the partners share profits in a _3 1_ ratio.

4 Carr and Davis agree to share profits in a 2 to 1 ratio after **allowing** salaries of $10,000 to Carr and $14,000 to Davis. Assuming that they earn only $6,000 **before** taking into account the salary allowances, Carr's share of the $6,000 profit will be $_4,000_ and Davis' share will be $_2,000_.

5 A partner invested an additional $4,000 in the partnership during Year 1. His share of partnership net income for Year 1 was $9,000, of which he withdrew only $2,000. The amount of partnership income that the partner must report on his personal income tax return is $_9,000_.

6 Among the disadvantages of the corporate form of organization are (a) _high taxes_ and (b) _regulation_.

7 Organization costs include (a) _chapter of corp_, (b) _issue expense of stock_, and (c) _underwriter_.

8 Directors of a corporation pass _____, which serve as a guide to the company's affairs. Subsequent actions by the board of directors and stockholders are recorded in the _____ book. Once a year most corporations issue an _____ _____ which includes the financial statements and other significant information relating to corporate activities.

9 The conversion of preferred stock into common generally requires a debit to _cash_

_____ and credits to _Preferred stock_ and a _credit to stock above Par Value_

10 A corporation had total assets of $400,000 and total liabilities of $150,000 at the beginning of Year 1. At the end of Year 1, it reported total assets of $600,000 and total liabilities of $200,000. During Year 1 it paid dividends of $48,000, representing 60% of its earnings. The total stockholders' equity at the end of Year 1 amounted to $_____, the earnings for Year 1 amounted to $_80,000_, and additional shares of capital stock were issued during Year 1 for $_____.

Multiple Choice

Choose the best answer for each of the following questions and enter the identifying letter in the space provided.

_____ **1** Periodic withdrawals by partners are best viewed as:
a Payment for partners' personal services to the partnership.
b Expenses of doing business.
c Decreases in the permanent capital of the partnership.
d Capital taken out of the business in anticipation of current earnings.

_____ **2** One of the following is **not** a characteristic of the corporate form of organization:
a Limited liability.
b Mutual agency.
c Centralized authority.
d Continuous existence.

_____ **3** Smith invests in a partnership land which cost his father $10,000. The land had a market value of $15,000 when Smith inherited it six years ago, and currently the land is conservatively appraised at $25,000 even though Smith insists that he "wouldn't take $50,000 for it." The land should be recorded in the accounts of the partnership at:
a $10,000   **c** $25,000
b $15,000   **d** $50,000

_____ **4** Partners X and Y have capital balances of $15,000 and $12,000, respectively. They share profits and losses in a 2 to 1 ratio. They sell all the partnership assets for $60,000, which results in a $6,000 gain. The amount that Y should receive as his share of cash upon liquidation of the partnership is:
a $12,000   **c** $14,000
b $20,000   **d** $23,000

5 Title to the assets of a corporation is legally held by:

a The stockholders, jointly and severally.

b The corporation, as a legal entity.

c The president of the corporation in trust for the stockholders.

d The board of directors, as trustees.

6 Which of the following is **not** a characteristic of most preferred stock issues?

a Preference as to dividends.

b Participating clause.

c Preference as to assets in event of liquidation.

d No voting power.

7 Which of the following is most relevant in determining the **cost** of assets acquired in exchange for capital stock?

a Par or stated value of the stock.

b Market value of the stock.

c Issuance price of stock already outstanding.

d Estimated useful life of the assets.

8 The Aaron Corporation is authorized to issue 100,000 shares of $10 par value capital stock. It issues one-half of the stock for $25 per share, earns $20,000 during the first three months of operation, and declares a cash dividend of $5,000. The total paid-in capital of the Aaron Corporation after three months of operation is:

a $1,000,000

b $1,250,000

c $1,020,000

d $1,265,000

9 One of the following is **not** an officer of a corporation:

a Stock registrar.

b Controller.

c Secretary.

d Treasurer.

10 When stock is sold on a subscription basis and the entire subscription price has been collected, the issuance of the stock is recorded by

a A debit to Cash and a credit to Capital Stock.

b A debit to Subscriptions Receivable: Capital Stock and a credit to Capital Stock Subscribed.

c A debit to Capital Stock Subscribed and a credit to Capital Stock.

d A debit to Capital Stock and a credit to Subscriptions Receivable: Capital Stock.

Exercises

1 A and B are partners, having capital balances at the beginning of Year 1 of $10,000 and $15,000, respectively.

Instructions: Indicate in the appropriate columns the division of partnership net income or net loss between the partners under the specified conditions.

If the division of net income results in a deduction from partners' capital, place parentheses around your answer to indicate this.

	A's Share	B's Share
First situation: Net income of the partnership is $10,000; partnership agreement provides for:		
a Net income to be divided in the ratio of beginning capitals..............	$ 4000	$ 6000
b Interest on beginning capitals at 6%; residual profit or loss divided 70% to A, 30% to B.............	$	$
c Interest on beginning capitals at 6%; salary to A of $4,000, to B of $3,000; residual profit or loss divided equally..........	$	$
Second situation: Net loss of the partnership is $4,000; partnership agreement:	$	$
a Is silent as to sharing profits or losses............		
b Provides salary to A of $7,000, salary to B of $5,000; residual profit or loss divided 40% to A and 60% to B.............	$	$

2 Ernst Corporation has outstanding 10,000 shares each of two classes of $100 par value stock: 5% cumulative preferred stock and common stock. The corporation reported a deficit of $20,000 at the beginning of Year 2, and preferred dividends have not been paid for one year. During Year 2 the corporation earned $180,000. How large a dividend per share did the corporation pay on the common stock if the balance in retained earnings at the end of Year 2 amounted to $25,000? Use the space below for computations.

3 Selected account balances for K and L, who share profits 60% to K and 40% to L, are shown below at the end of Year 1:

Account	Amount	
Income Summary	$15,000	(Cr)
K, Drawing	10,000	(Dr)
L, Drawing	4,000	(Dr)
K, Capital	18,400	(Cr)
L, Capital	17,750	(Cr)

a In the space below, prepare the closing entries required at the end of Year 1. Omit explanations.

General Journal		
Income Summary	15,000	
K Capital		18900
L Capital		17750
K Drawing		
L Drawing		
K Capital		
L Capital		

b Complete the partially filled-in statement of the partners' capitals shown below for Year 1, assuming that the partners did not invest additional capital in the business during the year.

K & L
Statement of Partners' Capitals
For Year 1

	K	L	Total
Balance, beginning of year..	$18,400	$17,750	$36,150
Add: Net income for year...	9000	6000	15000
Subtotal.	$27400	$23750	$51150
Less: Withdrawals.	10000	4000	14000
Balance, end of year.	$17400	$19750	$37150

4 Journalize the following transactions for Ozone Research, Inc., in the space provided below. Omit explanations.

a Paid $6,000 for costs of organizing the corporation.

b Issued 2,000 shares of $10 par capital stock in exchange for equipment valued at $30,000.

c Declared a cash dividend of 25 cents per share on 100,000 shares outstanding.

d Paid the dividend declared in transaction **c**.

	General Journal		
a			
b			
c			
d			

5 From the following account balances, prepare in good form the stockholders' equity section in the space provided:

Organization costs.	$ 7,000
Retained earnings.	128,000
Paid-in capital in excess of par: preferred	
stock.	10,000
Common stock, no-par value, 50,000 shares.	100,000
$4 preferred stock, $100 par, 1,000 shares. .	100,000

Receivable from underwriters (from sale of	
stock).	$ 40,000
Plant and equipment.	315,000
Accumulated depreciation.	125,000
Notes payable.	100,000

Stockholders' equity:
    $4 preferred stock, $100 par, 1,000
        shares issued and outstanding. $100,000

EIGHT

CORPORATIONS EARNINGS AND DIVIDENDS

HIGHLIGHTS OF THE CHAPTER

1 One of the most important aspects of corporate financial reporting is the measurement of periodic net income. *Earnings per share* reported over a period of years probably represent the most significant determinant of the market price of common stock and the amount of cash dividends per share.

2 The amount of annual and quarterly *earnings per share,* as well as the trend of such earnings, is closely watched by stockholders and security analysts. A record of steadily increasing earnings enables a company to raise new capital more readily and to retain competent management.

3 The *measurement of net income,* particularly the timing of revenue and expense recognition, has been a difficult task for accountants. In addition, the method of presenting nonoperating gains and losses in the income statement has been a controversial issue.

4 *APB Opinion No. 9* required the inclusion in the income statement of all items of profit and loss recognized during the period, except certain *prior period adjustments.* However, separate listing of extraordinary gains and losses was required. Gains and losses were not considered extraordinary if they were of a character typical of the customary business activity of the entity, and such gains and losses were to be included in the determination of income *before* extraordinary items.

5 *APB Opinion No. 30* established stricter guidelines for identifying and reporting extraordinary items and for measuring and reporting the operating results of discontinued segments of a business. Extraordinary gains and losses are much less frequently found in published financial statements today than was the case a few years ago.

6 A *segment of a business* is a component of a company whose activities represent a major line of business or class of customer. The assets and operating results of a segment should be easily identifiable from the other assets and operating results of the company.

7 The net operating results of a *discontinued segment* of a business for the current period should be reported separately in the income statement in arriving at the income before extraordinary items. Any gain or loss on the disposal of the segment is included in the *net* operating results of the discontinued segment.

8 The revenue and expenses shown in the income statement for the year in which a segment of a business is eliminated include *only the revenue and expenses from continuing operations.* The net income or loss from discontinued operations is reported separately; the total revenue from the discontinued segment is disclosed in the notes to the financial statements. Any gain or loss on the disposal of a segment should be reported with or near the results of discontinued operations and *not as an extraordinary item.*

9 Most companies realize gains and incur losses which are somewhat unrelated to the main activities of the company. Such gains and losses should be reported as extraordinary items only when the event or transaction is *unusual in nature and infrequent in occurrence* (considered in relation to the economic environment in which the company operates).

10 Only *unusual* and *infrequent* events and transactions result in extraordinary items to be reported below "income before extraordinary items" in the income statement. Some examples of extraordinary items are listed below:

a Effects of major casualties such as earthquake or flood (if rare in the area).

b Expropriation of assets by foreign governments.

c Effects of a prohibition under a newly enacted law or regulation.

11 To compute *earnings per share,* the net income for

a year or a quarter available to the common stock is divided by the number of shares outstanding. Investors use earnings per share in evaluating the past performance of a company and in forming an opinion as to its potential for future performance.

12 When a company has issued common stock only and the number of shares outstanding has not changed materially during the year, the amount of earnings per share is computed by dividing the net income for the year by the number of shares outstanding at year-end. When the number of shares outstanding has changed during the year as a result of issuance of shares for cash or other assets, the *weighted average number of shares outstanding* during the year must be determined by multiplying the number of shares outstanding by the fraction of the year that said number of shares outstanding remained unchanged.

13 When both nonconvertible preferred stock and common stock are outstanding, the amount of earnings per share of common stock is determined by dividing net income reduced by the amount of the current year's dividend on the preferred stock by the weighted average number of common shares outstanding during the year. Companies with a *complex capital structure* may present *dual* earnings per share, that is, *primary* and *fully diluted* earnings per share.

14 *Primary earnings per share* are based on the weighted average number of common shares actually outstanding plus common stock equivalents (stock options and other convertible securities which derive a significant part of their value from the conversion feature). *Fully diluted earnings per share* are based on the maximum potential number of shares outstanding. In computing earnings per share (both primary and fully diluted) the exercise of stock options and the conversion of bonds and preferred stocks into common stock is not *assumed* if the effect would be *antidilutive* (have the effect of increasing the earnings per share or decreasing a loss per share).

15 A *dividend* is generally understood to mean a pro rata cash distribution by a corporation to its stockholders. Dividends are declared by the board of directors after giving careful consideration to such factors as the balance in retained earnings and the company's cash position. Four dates are usually involved in the distribution of a dividend:
 a Date of declaration.
 b Date of record.
 c Ex-dividend date.
 d Date of payment.

16 Dividends are sometimes paid in a form other than cash, such as securities of other corporations or merchandise. A *liquidating dividend* usually takes place when a corporation goes out of business and distributes assets in final liquidation. A *stock dividend* is a distribution to stockholders of additional shares of the corporation's own common stock.

17 A stock dividend causes no change in assets or in the total amount of the stockholders' equity. The only effect of a stock dividend is to transfer a portion of the retained earnings into the Common Stock and the Paid-in Capital from Stock Dividends accounts. A stock dividend increases the number of common shares outstanding and decreases the book value per share. Each stockholder owns a larger number of shares after the stock dividend, but his total equity in the corporation remains unchanged.

18 What, then, are the reasons for distributing stock dividends? The reasons usually given are:
 a To conserve cash. During profitable years when business is expanding, a stock dividend is distributed in lieu of a cash dividend so that "profits" can be reinvested in the business.
 b To reduce the price per share of stock. When the price of a share of stock is high, a large stock dividend will reduce the price per share to a more convenient trading range.
 c To avoid income tax on stockholders. Stock dividends are not considered as taxable income to the recipients.

19 A "small" stock dividend may range from 1% of the outstanding stock to a maximum of 20 to 25%. Stock dividends of this size are recorded by a debit to Retained Earnings equal to the total *market value* of the additional shares being distributed, a credit to Stock Dividend to Be Distributed equal to the par or stated value of the additional shares, and a credit to Paid-in Capital from Stock Dividends equal to the excess of market value over par (or stated) value of the "dividend" shares. When the shares are distributed, Stock Dividend to Be Distributed is debited and Common Stock is credited.

20 Stock dividends in excess of, say, 20 to 25% are not considered "small" and are subject to different accounting treatment. They should be recorded by transferring only the *par* or *stated value* of the dividend shares from retained earnings to the Common Stock account.

21 A *stock split* is effected by reducing the par or stated value of the common stock and issuing a larger number of shares to each stockholder. In a 5 for 1 split, for example, the par value may be reduced from $10 to $2, and a shareholder owning 100 shares before the split would own 500 shares after the split.

22 If a company's net earnings since incorporation exceed the dividends declared, a credit balance appears in Retained Earnings; if losses have been incurred or if dividends have been paid in excess of total net income earned, a *deficit* appears in the Retained Earnings account.

23 *Prior period adjustments* are those material items of gain or loss which are directly related to the activities of a prior year and which could not have been measured with reasonable accuracy in the year of origin. In addition, prior period adjustments must not be attributable to an economic event of the current period and must be dependent on findings by persons other than management of the reporting corporation. Prior period adjustments are not included in the income statement but are shown in the retained earnings statement. Examples of prior period adjustments include additional tax assessments for prior years and settlements of lawsuits based on events of prior periods.

24 Retained earnings of a corporation are either "free" and available for dividends or "appropriated" (earmarked) for some specific purpose, such as to absorb possible losses or to show that retained earnings are not available for dividends because the funds generated by profitable operations are needed to finance expansion of plant facilities.

25 An appropriation of retained earnings is established by a debit to Retained Earnings and a credit to an appropriation account. The appropriation does not consist of cash or any other asset; it is simply a separate account reported within the stockholders' equity in the balance sheet. When the appropriation is no longer needed, it is returned to the Retained Earnings account by a debit to the appropriation account and a credit to Retained Earnings.

26 The statement of retained earnings reconciles the beginning balance in retained earnings with the ending balance. The usual format of the statement is to add (or deduct) any prior period adjustments to the beginning balance as originally reported. The restated beginning balance in retained earnings is then increased by the net income for the current year and reduced by the amount of dividends declared in arriving at the ending balance.

27 If a corporation acquires its own stock from stockholders, the reacquired stock is referred to as *treasury stock.* Treasury stock may be held indefinitely or may be reissued; it is not entitled to receive dividends or to vote.

28 Treasury stock is generally recorded at cost and is deducted from the total of the paid-in capital and retained earnings in the balance sheet. *Treasury*

stock is not an asset and no profit or loss is recognized on treasury stock transactions. When treasury stock is reissued, the Treasury Stock account is credited for the cost of the shares sold, and Paid-in Capital from Treasury Stock Transactions is credited (or debited) for the difference between cost and the reissuance price.

29 Corporations are not permitted to acquire treasury stock if such action would reduce legal capital. Thus retained earnings equal to the cost of treasury stock is restricted and is not available for declaration of cash dividends.

30 When only a single class of stock is outstanding, the *book value* per share is computed by dividing the total stockholders' equity by the number of shares outstanding. When both preferred and common stocks are outstanding, the book value per share of common stock is computed by dividing the number of shares of common stock into the common stockholders' equity (total stockholders' equity less the redemption value or call price of preferred stock).

TEST YOURSELF ON EARNINGS AND DIVIDENDS

True or False

For each of the following statements, circle the T or the F to indicate whether the statement is true or false.

T F **1** Prior period adjustments include all gains or losses which are not a part of the main activities of the business.

T F **2** Extraordinary items appear in the income statement and are included in the computation of total earnings per share.

T F **3** Both primary and fully diluted earnings per share are computed on the basis of the weighted average number of shares outstanding during the period.

T F **4** Common stock equivalents are not included in the weighted average number of shares outstanding for purposes of computing primary earnings per share if doing so would increase the reported earnings per share.

T F **5** When retained earnings are appropriated to cover a contingency, cash is set aside as a reserve to pay for the contingency if it occurs.

T   F   6 When an appropriation of retained earnings is no longer required, the appropriation (reserve) account is closed by a debit and an extraordinary gain account is credited.

T   F   7 Any cash received by a stockholder from the corporation in which he holds stock is properly referred to as a dividend.

T   F   8 The event or transaction resulting in an extraordinary loss must be both unusual in nature and infrequent in occurrence.

T   F   9 Growth companies are more likely to pay stock dividends than are companies with low or unstable profitability.

T   F   10 Stockholders must approve a dividend action taken by the board of directors.

T   F   11 A policy of paying regular quarterly dividends tends to give a higher investment (quality) rating to common stock.

T   F   12 A preferred stock with a par value of $25 paying a quarterly dividend of 37½ cents may be referred to as a "6% preferred" or as a "$1.50 preferred."

T   F   13 The investor who purchases shares of the X Co. on the "ex-dividend" date will not receive the next dividend paid by X Co.

T   F   14 A 3 for 1 stock split places stockholders of a company in essentially the same position as a 200% stock dividend.

T   F   15 A corporation's stockholders' equity accounts will be the same whether it declares a 100% stock dividend or splits its stock 2 for 1.

T   F   16 It may be argued that a stock dividend is not really a dividend since the corporation distributes no assets to its stockholders as a result of such action; however, stockholders welcome stock dividends and some corporations continue to distribute them as a regular policy.

T   F   17 A loss from a discontinued segment of a business should be reported below extraordinary items in the income statement.

T   F   18 The reissuance of treasury stock at a price in excess of the cost of these shares is a source of paid-in capital.

T   F   19 A corporation cannot acquire its own stock in the open market unless it has retained earnings at least equal to the purchase price.

T   F   20 The book value of a share of common stock is a valuable guide in judging the reasonableness of the market price of the stock, particularly for growth companies like Xerox and IBM.

Completion Statements

Fill in the necessary words or amounts to complete the following statements:

1 Large unexpected losses from inability to collect accounts receivable or from the shrinkage in the value of inventories should be taken into account in computing _____ before _____

_____ .

2 Companies with a complex capital structure generally report both _____ and _____

_____ earnings per share in the income statement.

3 Common stock equivalents may include the following: _____ , _____ _____ ,

and _____ _____ _____ .

4 Dividends in arrears on preferred stock are not reported as a liability in the balance sheet but should be disclosed by a _____ accompanying the financial statements.

5 On January 1, the Avery Corporation had 100,000 shares of capital stock with a par value of $10, additional paid-in capital of $300,000, and retained earnings of $700,000. During the year the company split its stock 2 for 1 (reducing the par value to $5 per share) and subsequently declared a 2% stock dividend (its first) when the market value of the stock was $40. It earned $200,000 during the year and paid no cash dividends. (a) At the end of the year the balance in the Capital Stock account will be $_____ ; (b) the balance in Additional Paid-in Capital will be $_____ ; and (c) the balance in Retained Earnings will be $_____ .

6 Given below is a list of accounts which appear in a balance sheet for a corporation:

Appropriation for puchase of treasury stock.	$ 20,000
Accumulated earnings—free.	780,000
Paid-in capital in excess of par.	317,400
Paid-in capital from stock dividends. . .	103,400
Stock dividend to be distributed (10%)	94,000
Treasury stock, 1,000 shares at cost. .	20,000 (debit)
Capital stock, $10 par value.	950,000
Paid-in capital from treasury stock transactions.	14,000
Cash dividends payable.	18,800
Appropriation for bond sinking fund. .	100,000

Complete the following: (a) Total of accumulated (retained) earnings, including appropriations, is $_____; (b) the latest cash dividend per share amounted to $_____; (c) treasury stock was acquired (before, after) _____ the declaration of the 10% stock dividend; (d) total stockholders' equity is $_____; (e) the market price of stock at the time the 10% stock dividend was declared was $_____ per share.

7 The book value of a share of capital stock is $10 per share. For each transaction or event listed below, use a check mark to indicate whether the transaction or event will increase, decrease, or have no effect on the book value per share of stock.

	Increase	Decrease	No Effect
a Declaration of cash dividend..........			
b Distribution of a 20% stock dividend......			
c A 4 for 1 stock split			
d Net income is reported for latest year.......			
e Additional stock is sold at $15.........			
f Treasury stock is acquired at $6 per share			
g Additional shares are authorized........			
h Par value of $5 per share is changed to stated value of $1 per share (not a split)....			

Multiple Choice

Choose the best answer for each of the following questions and enter the identifying letter in the space provided.

_____ **1** Which of the following is **least** important in determining the market value of a share of stock?
a Earnings and dividends per share.
b Book value per share.
c The available supply of the shares and the demand to purchase the shares.
d The par or stated value per share.

_____ **2** One of the following qualifies as an extraordinary item:
a Gain on sale of unprofitable consumer goods division.
b A large, unexpected write-off of an account receivable.
c A write-off and abandonment of goods in process inventory because of inability to get parts.
d Uninsured damages sustained on plant as a result of first flood in 30 years.

_____ **3** One of the following is **not** a prior period adjustment and should be reported in the income statement in arriving at income before extraordinary items:
a Tax deficiency applicable to a prior year.
b Retroactive settlement of litigation based on events of earlier periods.
c Settlement of rate disputes by public utilities.
d A substantial write-off of inventory because of rapid style change.

_____ **4** The book value per share of Price Company stock on January 1, 1977, was $31.50 per share. During 1977, the stock was split 3 for 1, and shortly afterward a 5% stock dividend was distributed. At the end of the year, a $1 cash dividend was declared and earnings per share of $3.10 were announced. The book value per share of stock as of December 31, 1977, amounted to:
a $10.50 b $10.70 c $12.10 d $13.10

_____ **5** The James Corporation had 100,000 shares of common stock and 5,000 shares of preferred stock outstanding at the beginning of Year 1. Each share of preferred stock was convertible into four shares of common stock (eight shares following the 2 for 1 split in November) and qualified as a common stock equivalent. On April 1, 10,000 shares of common stock were sold for cash and on November 3, the common stock was split 2 for 1. The weighted average number of shares outstanding for Year 1 in computing primary earnings per share is:
a 110,000 b 220,000 c 107,500 d 215,000
e 255,000

_____ **6** The distribution of a 20% stock dividend on common stock:
a Reduces the book value per share of common stock outstanding.
b Does not change the number of shares of common stock outstanding.
c Decreases total stockholders' equity.
d Increases the net assets of the corporation.

_____ **7** When a corporation declares a cash dividend on common stock, which of the following should be excluded in determining the **total amount** of the dividend?
a Shares issued in exchange for preferred stock.
b Shares held by officers and directors.
c Shares held by other corporations.
d Shares reacquired and held in treasury.

8 Revenue and expenses relating to a segment of business discontinued during the year are:

a Netted and reported as an extraordinary item.

b Included in total revenue and expenses as reported in the income statement.

c Netted and reported as a separate item of income before extraordinary items.

d Netted and reported as a prior period adjustment.

_____ **9** In recording a large stock dividend, say 50 or 100%, the amount of retained earnings transferred to paid-in capital is generally measured by:

a The market value of the stock on the date of declaration.

b The book value of the stock on the date of declaration.

c The par (or stated) value of the additional shares issued.

d The amount authorized by the board of directors to be transferred from the Retained Earnings account.

_____ **10** Treasury stock is best described as:

a Unissued stock.

b Temporarily retired stock which was previously outstanding.

c An asset acquired by making a cash disbursement.

d Retirement of a portion of outstanding stock which increases total stockholders' equity.

Exercises

1 From the following data for the Booker Company complete the statement of retained earnings for Year 10 by filling in the blanks provided:

Retained earnings as reported at end of Year 9.	$1,221,000
Net income.	294,000
Cash dividends.	40,000
Stock dividend (at market value).	150,000
Prior period adjustment—amount received in settlement of lawsuit initiated in Year 6.	375,000

BOOKER COMPANY

Statement of Retained Earnings

For Year 10

Retained earnings at beginning of year:		
As originally reported.		$1,221,000
Add: prior period adjustment—amount received in settlement of lawsuit initiated in Year 6.		375,000
As restated.		$ 1,596,000
Net income.		294,000
Subtotal.		$ 1,890,000
Less: Cash dividends.	$ 40,000	
Stock dividends.	150,000	190,000
Retained earnings at end of year.		$ 1,700,000

2 Given below is the stockholders' equity for the Lisbon Corporation on December 31, Year 5:

Stockholders' equity:		
8% cumulative preferred stock, $10 par, callable at $11 per share.		$ 200,000
Common stock, $5 stated value.		500,000
Paid-in capital in excess of par or stated value:		
Common stock.	$250,000	
Preferred stock.	10,000	260,000
Total paid-in capital.		$ 960,000
Retained earnings:		
Appropriated for purchase of treasury stock.	$ 17,500	
Unappropriated.	240,000	257,500
Total paid-in capital and retained earnings.		$1,217,500
Less: Cost of 2,000 shares of treasury stock (common).		17,500
Total stockholders' equity.		$1,200,000

From the information appearing in the stockholders' equity section of the balance sheet for the Lisbon Corporation, fill in the following blanks:

a Total legal capital amounts to $ 700000.

b The cost per share of treasury stock is $ 8.75.

c The issuance price per share of preferred stock is $ 10.50.

d The average issuance price per share of common stock is $ _7. 50_

e The book value per share of common stock is $_____.

3 At the beginning of Year 1, Bender Mfg. Company had 250,000 shares of $5 par value common stock outstanding. In the space provided below, prepare journal entries to record the following selected transactions during Year 1:

Mar. 1 Declared a cash dividend of 80 cents per share, payable on March 21.

Mar. 21 Paid cash dividend declared on March 1.

Aug. 10 Declared 5% stock dividend. The market price of the stock on this date was $40 per share.

Sept. 2 Issued 12,500 shares pursuant to 5% stock dividend declared on August 10.

Dec. 21 Declared and issued a 100% stock dividend. The market price of the stock on this date was $60 per share.

Dec. 30 Acquired 1,000 shares of its own common stock on the open market at $30 per share.

General Journal		
Year 1		
Mar. 1	Dividends	200000	
	Div. Payayable		200000
	Declared cash dividend of $0.80 per share on 250,000 shares.		
21	Div Payable	200000	
	Cash		200000
Aug. 10	R E	500000	
	C S Divide Dist.		62,500
	Premium		437,500
Sept. 2	C S D D	62,500	
	C / S		62,500
Dec. 21	R E	1,250,000	
	C/S		1,250,000
30	Treas. ~~Treasury Stock Common Stock~~	30,000	
	C ~~Treasury stock~~ Cash		30000

NINE

CASH AND MARKETABLE SECURITIES

HIGHLIGHTS OF THE CHAPTER

1 The term **cash** includes currency, coin, checks, money orders, and money on deposit with banks. Items which a bank will **not** accept for deposit such as postage stamps and postdated checks are **not** included in cash. Cash is a current asset and the most liquid of all assets. A company may have numerous bank accounts plus cash on hand, but these will be lumped together to show a single figure for cash in the balance sheet.

2 Management's job with respect to cash includes (a) preventing loss from fraud or theft; (b) accounting for cash receipts, cash payments, and cash balances; and (c) always having enough cash to make necessary payments, but not excessive cash deposits which produce no revenue. To meet these objectives, management needs a strong system of internal control.

3 Cash offers the greatest temptation to theft, and this makes the problem of internal control especially important. Basic rules to achieve strong internal control over cash include:

a Separating the handling of cash from the maintenance of accounting records.

b Separating the function of receiving cash from that of making cash disbursements.

c Depositing all cash receipts in the bank daily and making all payments by check.

d Keeping cash on hand under lock and obtaining fidelity bonds for all persons handling cash.

4 **Cash receipts** may be received over the counter from customers or through the mail. All cash received over the counter should be promptly recorded on a cash register in plain view of the customer. Prenumbered sales tickets should be prepared in duplicate whenever possible. The participation of two employees in each cash-receipts transaction is desirable. For example, one person opens the mail, prepares a list of checks received, and forwards one copy of the list to the accounting department and another copy with the checks to the cashier who will deposit them.

5 Good internal control over **cash disbursements** requires that all payments be made by prenumbered checks. The officials authorized to sign checks should not have authority to approve invoices for payment or to make entries in the accounting records. Before an official signs a check, he should require that supporting documents justifying the payment be presented to him. These documents should be stamped "Paid," and the checks should be mailed without going back to the person who prepared them.

6 In opening a bank checking account, the depositor must leave a **signature card** on file at the bank. Deposit tickets should be prepared in duplicate for each deposit made, with the duplicate being retained by the depositor.

7 Each month the bank will provide the depositor with a **statement** of his account, showing the beginning balance, dates and amounts of deposits, deductions for checks paid, any other charges, and the ending balance. All paid checks are returned to the depositor with the bank statement. When numerous checks are being deposited daily, it is inevitable that occasionally one will **bounce,** that is, the drawer of the check will have insufficient funds on deposit to cover it. The check will be marked NSF (not sufficient funds), charged back against the depositor's account, and returned to him. An NSF check should be regarded as a receivable rather than cash, until it is collected directly from the drawer, redeposited, or determined to be worthless.

8 The amount of cash which appears on the balance sheet of a business should be the correct amount of cash owned at the close of business on that date. To determine this amount, it is necessary to **reconcile** the monthly bank statement with the balance of cash as shown by the depositor's accounting records. The balance shown on the bank statement will usually not agree with that shown on the depositor's books because certain transactions will have been recorded by one party but not by the other. Examples are outstanding checks, deposits in transit, service charges, NSF checks, and errors by the bank or by the depositor.

9 The **bank reconciliation** will identify the items which cause the balance of cash per the books to differ from the balance shown on the bank statement and will show the adjusted or correct amount of cash. Those reconciling items which have not yet been recorded by the depositor (or which reflect errors on his part) must be entered on the books to make the accounting records correct and up to date at the end of the period.

10 As previously stressed, it is desirable that all cash payments be made by check; however, in every business some small expenditures are necessary for which it is not practicable to issue checks. Taxi fares, collect telegrams, and postage stamps are common examples. To control these small payments not being made by check, almost every business establishes a **petty cash fund.** A check is written for perhaps $50 or $100 and is cashed, and the cash is kept on hand for use in making small expenditures. A receipt or **petty cash voucher** should be obtained and placed in the fund to replace each cash payment. Therefore the fund always contains a constant amount of cash and vouchers. The expenses are recorded in the accounts when the fund is replenished, perhaps every two or three weeks. The entry for the replenishment check will consist of debits to the proper expense accounts and a credit to Cash.

11 Many companies invest cash not needed for current operations in government bonds and securities issued by other corporations. These investments in **marketable securities** are readily convertible back into cash. In the meanwhile, such investments are preferable to holding idle cash because of the interest or dividend revenue which they produce.

12 A special tax incentive exists to encourage corporations to invest in the capital stock of other corporations; 85% of most dividend revenue earned by a corporation is not subject to federal income tax.

13 Investments in marketable securities should be considered current assets, providing that they are **readily marketable.** This means that (a) the securities can be converted into cash without disrupting the normal operations of the business, and (b) a **ready market** exists for the security at quoted market prices. However, if securities of other corporations are held in sufficient quantity that a

degree of control may be exercised over the issuing corporation, such investments could not be sold without disrupting established policies, and they are not classified as current assets. Securities held for **purposes of control** may be listed under the heading of **Investments,** instead of **Current Assets.**

14 Investments in marketable securities are usually carried at cost with a parenthetical note in the balance sheet showing their current market value. Another acceptable valuation method is to carry these assets at the lower of cost or market.

15 Many accountants are convinced that investments in securities **should be** valued in the balance sheet at **current market price.** This value is the most significant to the banker or other user of the balance sheet in judging financial strength and debt-paying ability. Moreover, the market value is readily obtainable and can be objectively verified.

16 One problem in revaluing investments in marketable securities for fluctuations in current market prices is that the corresponding gain or loss **has not been realized** by a completed transaction. The alternative methods which might be used to account for this unrealized gain or loss are discussed and illustrated in your textbook. **Remember,** valuation of marketable securities at current market price is **not** in accordance with current accounting practice.

17 For income tax purposes, no gain or loss is recognized on an investment in securities until the time of sale.

18 Since cost is the major factor in establishing the valuation of securities, we need a clear understanding of the way cost is measured. Commissions paid to a broker for purchase of securities are included in cost of the investment. Bond prices are quoted as a percentage of their maturity (par) value. Thus, a price of 92 means $920 market price for a bond with a $1,000 maturity value. Stock prices are quoted in terms of dollars per share.

19 Most corporate bonds pay interest semiannually; when an investor buys bonds at any time between these interest payment dates, he pays the current market price of the bond plus the interest accrued since the last semiannual interest payment. This added payment for interest is not part of the cost of the bond but is debited to a separate account and collected as part of the next semiannual interest payment from the issuing corporation. Interest accrues from day to day on bonds, but dividends do not accrue on stock. Usually dividends are not recognized as earned until the date of receipt.

20 Gains and losses on the sale of marketable securities, as well as interest and dividends earned, are all nonoperating income. These items should be shown separately on the income statement after the determination of income from operations.

TEST YOURSELF ON
CASH AND MARKETABLE SECURITIES

True or False

For each of the following statements, circle the T or the F to indicate whether the statement is true or false.

T F 1 The balance sheet item of Cash includes amounts on deposit with banks, and also currency, money orders, and customers' checks on hand.

T F 2 Reconciling a bank account means determining that all deductions shown on the bank statement represent checks issued by the depositor in the current period.

T F 3 No entry is made in the accounting records at the time a small payment is made from the petty cash fund.

T F 4 Internal control over cash should include measures to prevent fraud or loss, to provide accurate records of cash transactions, and to assure the maintenance of adequate but not excessive cash balances.

T F 5 Internal control over cash receipts is most effective when one person is made solely responsible for receiving and depositing cash and making related entries in the accounting records.

T F 6 All cash receipts should be deposited intact in the bank daily, and all cash payments should be made by check.

T F 7 The purpose of preparing a bank reconciliation is to identify those items which cause the balance of cash per the bank statement to differ from the balance of cash per the ledger, and thereby to determine the correct cash balance.

T F 8 In preparing a bank reconciliation, outstanding checks should be deducted from the balance shown on the bank statement, and deposits in transit (or undeposited receipts) should be added to the bank balance.

T F 9 James Company deposited a check from a customer, Ray Prince, but the bank returned the check with the notation NSF and deducted it on James Company's bank state-

ment. A telephone call to Prince's office indicated that he would be out of town for some weeks. James Company decided to hold the check until Prince returned. The check should be included in the figure for Cash on the balance sheet of James Company.

T F 10 The Petty Cash account should be debited when the fund runs low and a check is drawn to replenish the fund.

T F 11 After preparing a bank reconciliation, journal entries should be made to record each of the items shown as adjustments to the balance per depositor's records.

T F 12 A recent balance sheet of Sears, Roebuck and Co. showed among the current assets the item of Marketable Securities. The cost of the securities was approximately $1⅓ million and the current market value was approximately $30 million. Under generally accepted accounting principles, the marketable securities would be shown at their cost with a parenthetical note about their current market value.

T F 13 The quoted market price of marketable securities is established every morning by an agency of the federal government.

T F 14 Application of the lower-of-cost-or-market rule to investments in marketable securities will produce a more conservative balance sheet valuation if applied on an item-by-item basis.

T F 15 Investments in marketable securities should not be classified as current assets unless management clearly states an intention to sell them within the next year.

T F 16 Jay Corporation purchased government bonds at a cost of $1 million, but at the next balance sheet date the market value of the bonds had dropped to $950,000. If Jay Corporation reduces the carrying value of the bonds to market, it may deduct the $50,000 loss on its income tax return.

T F 17 A company which invests in bonds and stocks should make an adjusting entry at year-end to accrue interest on bonds and dividends on any preferred stocks owned.

T F 18 A small retail store invested in 100 shares of General Motors stock. This stock should be classified as a current asset on the store's balance sheet even though management has no intention of selling the stock within the next year.

T F 19 One reason that marketable securities are valued at original cost instead of current market price is that the related gain or loss has not been realized by a completed transaction.

 T *F* **20** The use of an Unrealized Gain or Loss account in the stockholders' equity section of the balance sheet is an alternative to including unrealized gains and losses in the income statement.

Completion Statements

Fill in the necessary words or amounts to complete the following statements:

1 The term **cash** includes not only currency, coin, and money orders, but also _____ and _____.

2 An adequate system of internal control over cash should include separating the function of handling cash from the _____ _____ _____ _____.

3 Internal control is also strengthened if the function of receiving cash collections is separated from the function of making _____ _____.

4 Cash frauds often begin with temporary unauthorized "borrowing" by employees of cash received from customers. One effective step in preventing such irregularities is to insist that each day's cash receipts be _____ _____ _____ _____ : _____.

5 If duties relating to cash handling and the maintenance of accounting records are sufficiently subdivided so that the work of one person or department serves to verify that of another, then the permanent concealment of fraud is possible only through the _____ _____ _____ _____ _____ _____.

6 Among the most common reconciling items in a bank reconciliation are _____ _____, which should be deducted from the balance shown by the bank, and _____ _____ _____, which should be added to the balance shown by the bank statement.

7 The abbreviation **NSF** applied to a check returned by a bank means _____ _____ _____, and calls for an entry on the depositor's books debiting _____ _____ _____.

8 In the preparation of a bank reconciliation, various reconciling items are added to or deducted from the balance per the bank statement or the balance per the depositor's records. Outstanding checks should be _____ _____ the balance per the _____ _____ _____. Deposits in transit should be _____ _____ the balance per the _____ _____ _____. Bank service charges should be _____ _____ the balance per the _____ _____. Collections made by the bank in behalf of the depositor should be _____ _____ the balance per the _____ _____.

9 For each 8%, 20-year bond issued, the X Company received $925. The market quotation as shown in the newspaper for these bonds would be _____.

10 When an investor purchases bonds between interest dates, the excess of his payment over the price of the bond and the commission will be debited to an account entitled _____ _____ _____ _____.

11 Dividends in the form of additional shares of stock are not _____ to the stockholder, but do decrease his _____ _____ per share.

12 Toma Company plans to write up its investment in marketable securities to a current market price greater than cost. The journal entry to record this revaluation could be done either of two ways: by _____ the Investment account and either _____ _____ _____ _____ or _____ _____ _____. _____ (Both, Only one, Neither) of these methods is currently acceptable accounting practice.

Multiple Choice

Choose the best answer for each of the following questions and enter the identifying letter in the space provided.

_____ **1** The X Company maintains four **separate** bank accounts, of which three are in local banks and the fourth in a major New York City bank. The company also maintains a $300 petty cash fund. In the year-end balance sheet, cash should be reported by:

a Showing separately the amount of each bank account and the petty cash fund and also showing a total figure representing the combined amount of cash on deposit and the petty cash fund.

b Showing the total of the four bank accounts as a

single amount and listing the petty cash fund as a separate item.

c Showing the total of the three local bank accounts separately from the New York City bank account and the petty cash fund.

d Showing a single amount for cash including the four bank accounts and the petty cash fund.

_c_ 2 Which of the following practices is undesirable from the standpoint of maintaining adequate internal control over cash?

a Recording overages and shortages from errors in handling over-the-counter cash receipts in a ledger account, Cash Over and Short.

b Authorizing the cashier to make bank deposits.

c Authorizing the official who approves invoices for payment to sign checks.

d Appointing as custodian of a petty cash fund an employee who has no responsibility with respect to maintenance of accounting records.

_c_ 3 Checks received through the mail should be:

a Transmitted to the accounts receivable department without delay.

b Deposited by the mail-room employee.

c Listed by the mail-room employee and forwarded to the cashier; a copy of the list should be sent to the accounts receivable department.

d Handled first by the accounts receivable department, which after making appropriate entries in the accounts should turn over the checks to the cashier to be made part of the daily bank deposit.

_c_ 4 When a bank reconciliation has been satisfactorily completed, the only related entries to be made on the depositor's books are:

a To correct errors existing in the accounts.

b To record outstanding checks and bank service charges.

c To record items which explain the difference between the balance per the books and the adjusted cash balance.

d To reconcile items which explain the difference between the balance per the books and the balance per the bank statement.

_a_ 5 In establishing and maintaining a petty cash fund:

a The Petty Cash account is debited only when the fund is first established or subsequently changed in size.

b The Petty Cash account is debited whenever the fund is replenished.

c The contents of the fund should at all times be limited to currency, coin, and checks.

d The contents of the fund should at all times be limited to currency, coin, checks, money orders,

undeposited cash receipts, petty cash vouchers, and notes receivable from employees.

_b_ 6 An NSF check held by the payee should be carried on its records as:

a An element of cash on hand.

b Notes receivable.

c Accounts receivable.

d Cash over and short.

_c_ 7 Which of the following is not a significant element of internal control over cash disbursements?

a Perforating or stamping "Paid" on supporting invoices and vouchers.

b Using serially numbered checks and accounting for all numbers in the series.

c Use of a Cash Over and Short account.

d Establishment of a petty cash fund.

_b_ 8 Which of the following is not a significant element of internal control over cash receipts?

a Prelisting customers' remittances received in the mail.

b Establishing a petty cash fund.

c Depositing each day's cash receipts intact in the bank.

d Prenumbering sales tickets.

_a_ 9 Corporations generally invest in government bonds and securities of other corporations in order to:

a Avoid paying income taxes on their entire earnings.

b Derive some revenue and possible appreciation while maintaining resources which can readily be converted into cash.

c Avoid distributing an excessive portion of earnings as dividends.

d Offset earnings from investments against operating losses.

_a_ 10 When investments in securities are sold, any gain or loss should be:

a Shown on the income statement after the figure representing income from operation.

b Debited or credited directly to the Retained Earnings account to avoid confusing these gains and losses with operating results.

c Recorded by a debit to Cash, a debit to Commission Expense, and a credit to Sales.

d Recorded by entries in the accounts for Cash, Commissions Expense, and Gain or Loss on Sale of Investments.

_c_ 11 The valuation of investments in marketable securities:

a Is based on cost rather than current market value because bankers, creditors, and other users of the balance sheet are more interested in original cost of the investment than in its present market value.

b May under present standards of accounting practice

properly be on the basis of cost, or on the basis of the lower of cost or market.

c Is usually based on cost because an increase in carrying value to reflect higher market prices would require the payment of income taxes on the amount of the write-up.

d Is usually based on cost because of the practical difficulties in obtaining objective verification of current market value.

b 12 Dart Co. bought $10,000 (maturity value) of 8% bonds at a price of 92. The brokerage commission was $30 and accrued interest amounted to $200. Dart Co. should debit Investment in Bonds:

a $9,200

b $9,230

c $9,430

d Some other amount.

Exercises

1 You are to fill in the missing portions of the bank reconciliation shown on this page for the Hunter Corporation at July 31, 19____, using the following additional information:

a Outstanding checks: no. 301, $2,500; no. 303, $600; no. 304, $1,800, no. 306, $1,282.

b Service charge by bank, $6.

c Deposit made after banking hours on July 31, $1,950.

d A $264 NSF check drawn by our customer Jay Kline, deducted from our account by bank and returned to us.

e An $1,800 note receivable left by us with bank for collection was collected and credited to our account. No interest involved.

f Our check no. 295, issued in payment for $580 of office supplies, was erroneously written as $688 but was recorded in our accounts as $580.

HUNTER CORPORATION
Bank Reconciliation
July 31, 19____

Balance per depositor's records, July 31, 19____	$11,364
Add: *DIT NR*	~~1950~~ 1800
	~~13314~~ 108
Deduct: *Check Error*	13272 1908
O/S 301 2500	
303 600 NSF 264	
304 1800 SC 6	270
306 1282	6182

Adjusted balance.	~~$7132~~ 13002
Balance per bank statement, July 31, 19____. . .	$17,018
Add: *NR* *DIT*	~~1800~~ 1950
Check error	108
Deduct:	19968
NSF 264	
BSC 6	
O/S Check	6182

Adjusted balance (as above). $13786

2 Prepare the necessary journal entries based on the information in the bank reconciliation of the Hunter Corporation in Exercise 1.

	General Journal		
19____			
June 30			

3 On September 1, 1976, National Company bought $100,000 par value of World Airlines 6% bonds of 1998 at a price of 87¾ and accrued interest, plus a brokerage commission of $500. Interest dates of the bonds were August 1 and February 1. On April 1, 1977, the National Company sold the bonds at a price of 91.

Complete the journal entries for the several transactions relating to the bonds as indicated below.

1976	General Journal		
Sept. 1	Accrued Bond Interest Receivable		
	Purchased $100,000 par value of World Airlines 6% bonds of 1998,		
	at 87¾ and accrued interest, plus commission of $500.		
Dec. 31			
	To accrue bond interest earned to Dec. 31 ($100,000 × 6% × 4/12).		
1977			
Feb. 1			
	Received semiannual bond interest on World Airlines bonds ($100,000		
	× 6% × ½).		
Apr. 1			
	To accrue interest to date of sale of investment in World Airlines		
	bonds ($100,000 × 6% × 2/12).		
Apr. 1			
	To record sale of $100,000 par value of World Airlines 6% bonds of		
	1998 at 91 plus accrued interest of $1,000 and minus commission		
	of $500.		

RECEIVABLES AND PAYABLES

TEN

HIGHLIGHTS OF THE CHAPTER

1 An important factor in the growth of the American economy has been the increasing tendency to sell goods on credit. In most large businesses, the major portion of total sales are actually sales on credit. Since every credit sale creates some sort of receivable from the customer, it follows that accounts receivable and/or notes receivable will be large and important assets on the balance sheets of most businesses.

2 A business can increase sales by giving its customers easy credit terms. But no business wants to sell on credit to a customer who will be unable to pay his account. Consequently, many businesses have a credit department which investigates the credit record of each new customer to see if he is an acceptable credit risk.

3 A few accounts receivable will prove to be uncollectible. As long as the portion of uncollectible accounts is relatively small, it is to the advantage of the business to go ahead and incur these losses because the extension of credit to customers is also bringing in a lot of profitable business. The losses from accounts that do prove uncollectible are an *expense* resulting from using credit to increase sales.

4 A most fundamental accounting principle is that *revenue must be matched with the expenses incurred in securing that revenue.* Uncollectible Accounts Expense is caused by selling goods or services to customers who fail to pay their bills. The expense is therefore incurred in the period the sale is made even though the receivable is not determined to be uncollectible until some following period. At the end of each accounting period before preparing financial statements, we must therefore *estimate* the amount of uncollectible accounts expense. This estimate is brought on the books by an adjusting entry debiting *Uncollectible Accounts Expense* and crediting *Allowance for Uncollectible Accounts.* The Allowance for Uncollectible Accounts is a *contra-asset account;* it appears in the

balance sheet as a deduction from Accounts Receivable and thus leads to an *estimated realizable value* for receivables.

5 Allowance for Uncollectible Accounts is sometimes called *Allowance for Bad Debts.* Uncollectible Accounts Expense is sometimes referred to as *Bad Debts Expense.*

6 Since the allowance for uncollectible accounts is necessarily an estimate rather than a precise calculation, there is a fairly wide range of reasonableness within which the amount may be set. The factor of conservatism which historically has been of considerable influence on accounting practice implies a tendency to state assets at their minimum values rather than in a purely objective manner. Establishing a relatively large allowance for uncollectible accounts also means recording a relatively large amount of uncollectible accounts expense, and thus tending to minimize net income for the current period.

7 Two methods of estimating uncollectible accounts expense are in wide use. The first method, which we call the *balance sheet approach,* relies on aging the *accounts receivable* and thereby arriving at the total amount estimated to be uncollectible. The allowance for uncollectible accounts is then adjusted (usually increased) to this estimated probable expense, after *giving consideration to the existing balance* in the allowance account.

8 The alternative method of estimating uncollectible accounts expense stresses that the *expense* is usually a fairly constant *percentage of sales* (or of sales on credit). Therefore the amount of the adjustment is computed as a percentage of the period's sales *without regard to any existing balance* in the allowance account. This method is often called the *income statement approach* to estimating uncollectible accounts expense.

9 An *aging schedule* for accounts receivable is a list of the balances due from all customers, with each amount placed in a column indicating its age. Thus, we might use columns with headings such as Not Yet Due, Past Due 1 to 30 Days, Past Due 31 to 60 Days, etc. Each column total should be computed

as a percentage of total receivables. Changes in the percentages from month to month indicate whether the quality of receivables is improving or deteriorating.

10 When a customer's account is determined to be uncollectible, it should immediately be written off. The write-off consists of a debit to the Allowance for Uncollectible Accounts and a credit to Accounts Receivable. The credit will be posted to the customer's account in the subsidiary ledger as well as to the controlling account in the general ledger. Since the write-off reduces both the asset Accounts Receivable, and the contra-asset Allowance for Uncollectible Accounts, **there is no change in the net carrying value of receivables.** Neither is there any recognition of expense at the time of the write-off. The write-off merely confirms the validity of our earlier estimate in recording uncollectible accounts expense in the period the sale was made.

11 The **direct charge-off method** of recognizing uncollectible accounts expense does not recognize any expense until a particular account receivable is determined to be uncollectible. At that point the receivable is written off with an offsetting debit to Uncollectible Accounts Expense. An allowance account is not used. There is little theoretical support for the direct charge-off method because it makes no attempt to match revenue with the expenses associated with that revenue. This method is not widely used.

12 Making credit sales to customers who use major credit cards avoids the risk of uncollectible accounts because the account receivable is paid promptly by the credit card company. Making sales through credit card companies also has the advantages of eliminating the work of credit investigations, billing, and maintaining an accounts receivable subsidiary ledger. However, credit card companies charge a fee equal to a percentage (usually 3 to 7%) of each credit sale.

13 In analyzing financial statements it is common practice to consider the relationship between average receivables and annual credit sales. For example, if annual credit sales were $2,400,000 and average receivables were $600,000, receivables would represent one-fourth of a year's sales (90 days' sales). If the credit terms are, say, 30 days, it is apparent that many receivables are past due, that the **turnover** of receivables is too slow, and that corrective action is needed.

14 **Installment sales** typically require a small down payment and a long series of monthly payments, perhaps extending over several years. For income tax purposes, a business is permitted to spread the profit on an installment sale over the period of collection in proportion to the cash received. For financial statements, however, the installment basis of measuring income has been prohibited by the American Institute of Certified Public Accountants. The principle of matching revenue with related expenses is best achieved by recognizing the entire gross profit in the period of the sale and by establishing an allowance for uncollectible accounts.

15 A promissory note is an unconditional promise in writing to pay on demand or at a future date a definite sum of money. Most notes are for periods of a year or less and are therefore classified as current assets by the payee and as current liabilities by the maker of the note. Most notes bear interest (a charge made for the use of money). Interest rates are stated on an annual basis and a 360-day year is usually assumed. The formula is: **Principal × rate of interest × time** equals interest. *(Prt = i.)*

16 The **60-day, 6% method** is a shortcut method for computing interest. The interest for 60 days at 6% on any sum of money can be computed merely by moving the decimal point two places to the left.

17 All notes receivable are usually posted to a single account in the general ledger at their face amount. The notes themselves when properly filed are the equivalent of a subsidiary ledger. An adjusting entry for interest accrued on notes receivable is necessary at the end of the period. The entry will debit Accrued Interest Receivable and will credit Interest Earned. When the note is collected in the following period, the entry will be a debit to Cash offset by a credit to Notes Receivable for the face amount of the note, a credit to Accrued Interest Receivable for the amount of the accrual, and a credit to Interest Earned for the remainder of the interest collected.

18 If the maker of the note defaults (fails to pay as agreed), an entry should be made to transfer the note and any interest earned to an account receivable. If both parties agree that a note should be renewed rather than paid at maturity, an entry should be made debiting and crediting the Notes Receivable account.

19 Notes receivable are often **discounted,** that is, sold to a financial institution, with the seller endorsing the note and thereby agreeing to make payment if the maker defaults.

20 When a businessman endorses a note and discounts it to a bank, he promises to pay the bank if the maker of the note fails to do so. This liability of the endorser is known as a **contingent liability.** A contingent liability is a potential liability which will either develop into a real liability or be eliminated, depending upon some future event. Contingent liabilities are disclosed in **footnotes** to the balance sheet, not in the regular liability section.

21 **Current liabilities** are amounts payable to creditors within one year or the operating cycle, whichever is longer. A company's debt-paying ability is judged, in part, by the relationship of its current assets to its current liabilities. Some examples of current liabilities are notes payable, accounts payable, cash dividends payable, and various types of accrued liabilities.

22 A note payable may be issued as evidence of indebtedness to banks or to other creditors. When money is borrowed from the bank, two approaches may be used in drawing up the note: (a) The note is drawn for the **principal amount**, and interest is stated separately, to be paid at maturity. (b) The note is drawn for the **amount borrowed plus the interest to be paid at maturity.** When this procedure is followed, the rate of interest (or the amount of interest) is not separately listed on the note.

23 When the note is drawn for the principal amount borrowed, Cash is debited and Notes Payable is credited at the time the note is issued. The entry to record the payment of principal and interest requires a debit to Notes Payable for the amount of principal, a debit to Interest Expense for the interest paid, and a credit to Cash.

24 When the note is drawn for the **amount being borrowed plus the interest,** the note is for an amount larger than the immediate liability because the note includes interest **not yet owed** to the creditor. When such a note is drawn, Cash is debited for the amount received, **Discount on Notes Payable** is debited for the interest not yet owed, and Notes Payable is credited for the face amount of the note. Discount on Notes Payable is a **contra-liability** account, and is subtracted from Notes Payable on the balance sheet, so that the net liability reflects only the amount owed at present.

25 When the note is paid, the interest has been earned by the creditor. The balance of the Discount on Notes Payable account is therefore recognized as interest expense (debit Interest Expense; credit Discount on Notes Payable). Notes Payable is debited and Cash is credited to record the payment of the note.

26 If a note is not repaid in the same period it was issued, it will be necessary to recognize the interest which has accrued (become owed) on the note during each period. If the note is drawn only for the principal amount, the interest which has accrued during the period is recognized by a debit to Interest Expense, and a credit to the liability account Accrued Interest Payable. If the interest was included in the face of the note, the interest which accrues each period is transferred from Discount on Notes Payable (interest not yet owed) to Interest Expense. This entry would debit Interest Expense and credit (reduce) the contra-liability account Discount on Notes Payable.

27 When a note receivable is drawn to include future interest charges in the face amount of the note, the amount of the unearned interest should be credited to a **contra-asset** account entitled **Discount on Notes Receivable.** The interest which is earned each period is then transferred from Discount on Notes Receivable (representing the unearned interest) to the revenue account Interest Earned. The journal entry would debit (reduce) the contra-asset account Discount on Notes Receivable and credit Interest Earned.

28 When no interest rate or amount is stated, a portion of any long-term note (receivable or payable) should be assumed to represent an interest charge. Treating a portion of the face amount of a note as interest is termed **imputing** the interest.

29 Because interest payments are deductible for income tax purposes, some businessmen pay in advance the interest on notes payable. In such cases, the effective rate of interest on the money borrowed is higher than the rate agreed upon. This is true because the amount of interest paid is the same whether paid in advance or at maturity, but if the businessman pays in advance, he has the use of less money during the life of the note.

TEST YOURSELF ON RECEIVABLES AND PAYABLES

True or False

For each of the following statements, circle the T or the F to indicate whether the statement is true or false.

 1 The practice of estimating uncollectible accounts expense at the end of each accounting period is designed to match revenue and expenses so that all expenses associated with the revenue earned in the period are recognized as expense in that same period.

 2 During the first year of its existence, Cross Company made most of its sales on credit but made no provision for uncollectible accounts. The result would be an overstatement of assets and owners' equity, an understatement of expense, and an overstatement of net income.

T F 3 Conservatism in the valuation of accounts receivable would call for holding the amount entered in Allowance for Uncollectible Accounts to a bare minimum.

T F 4 The **balance sheet** approach to estimating uncollectible accounts expense emphasizes the aging of accounts receivable and the adjustment of the allowance account to the level of the estimated uncollectible amount.

T F 5 The **income statement** approach to estimating uncollectible accounts expense does not require the use of an allowance account.

T F 6 When the year-end provision for uncollectible accounts expense is estimated as a percentage of sales, the estimate is recorded without regard for the existing balance in the allowance account.

T F 7 The **direct charge-off** method does not cause receivables to be stated in the balance sheet at their estimated realizable value.

T F 8 When a given account receivable is determined to be worthless, it should be written off the books by an entry debiting Uncollectible Accounts Expense and crediting the Allowance for Uncollectible Accounts.

T F 9 When a company collects an account receivable previously written off as worthless, an entry should be made debiting Accounts Receivable and crediting Allowance for Uncollectible Accounts. A separate entry is then made to record collection of the account.

T F 10 The write-off of an account receivable determined to be worthless by debiting the Allowance for Uncollectible Accounts will not affect the net carrying value of the receivables in the balance sheet.

T F 11 Annual credit sales divided by the amount of average accounts receivable indicates how long it takes to convert receivables into cash.

T F 12 The installment basis of recognizing revenue on installment sales is accepted for income tax purposes and conforms to the accounting principle of matching revenue with related expenses.

T F 13 A retailer who sells to a customer using a national credit card will have an uncollectible account if the customer never pays the credit card company.

T F 14 When a company accepts an interest-bearing note from a customer, the accounting entry should include a debit for the principal plus the interest specified in the note.

T F 15 The interest on a 6%, 60-day note for any amount can be computed merely by moving the decimal point two places to the left; if the note is for 90 days, the computed amount of interest is merely increased by one-half.

T F 16 When a non-interest-bearing note receivable is discounted with a bank, the cash proceeds will usually be equal to the maturity value of the note.

T F 17 Interest may be stated separately or included in the face amount of a note payable.

T F 18 In reporting notes payable in the balance sheet, the Discount on Notes Payable account should be subtracted from the balance in the Notes Payable account.

T F 19 If the interest is not included in the face amount of a note payable, accrued interest at the end of a period should be recognized in a separate liability account; if the interest is included in the face amount, accrued interest should be recognized by decreasing the Discount on Notes Payable account.

T F 20 Contingent liabilities may not become real liabilities and need not be disclosed in the financial statements or footnotes to the statements.

T F 21 If goods are sold in exchange for a long-term, non-interest-bearing note receivable, failure to impute interest will cause an overstatement of assets, net income, and owners' equity.

Completion Statements

Fill in the necessary words or amounts to complete the following statements:

1 The accounting principle which underlies the practice of estimating uncollectible accounts expense each period is known as _____ _____ _____ _____. This process is essential to the periodic determination of _____ _____.

2 If the Allowance for Uncollectible Accounts is understated, the net realizable value of accounts receivable will be _____, owners' equity will be _____, and net income will be _____.

3 The income statement approach to uncollectible accounts emphasizes estimating _____ _____ _____ for the period, while the balance sheet approach emphasizes estimating the proper level for the

_____ _____

_____.

4 Bitterroot Company obtained a $16,000 note receivable from a customer and discounted it at the bank the same day, receiving a sum of $15,940. The entry to record the discounting would be a

debit to Cash for $_____, a _____

to _____ _____ for $_____,

and a credit to Notes Receivable for $_____.

5 If the interest on a 60-day note with a face value of $10,000 amounts to $125, the rate of interest is

_____% per annum.

6 The entry to record interest accrued on notes receivable at the year-end consists of a debit to

_____ _____

and a credit to _____ _____
Of these accounts, the one to be closed into the

Income Summary is _____

_____.

7 The Inn Place made credit sales of $4,200 to customers using Global Express credit cards. Global Express charges retailers a fee of 4%. The entry to record collecting the cash from these credit sales

would be a debit to Cash for $_____, a

_____ to _____

for $_____, and a _____ to _____

_____ for $_____.

8 Discount on Notes Payable is a _____

_____ account which should be _____
from the face value of notes payable in the liability section of the balance sheet. The amount of the Discount on Notes Payable will eventually be

recognized as _____ _____.

9 Discount on Notes Receivable is a _____

_____ account which should be _____

from the face value of _____ _____.
The amount of the Discount on Notes Receivable will

eventually be recognized as _____

_____.

10 Company A borrows $10,000 cash and signs a note for $10,150, due in 60 days. On the same day, Company B borrows $10,000 cash and signs a note for $10,000 plus 9% interest, due in 60 days. Thirty days after borrowing the money, both companies prepared financial statements. The liability relating

to the loan for Company A (Notes Payable less remaining Discount on Notes Payable) would be

$_____; the liability for Company B (Notes Payable plus Accrued Interest Payable) would be

$_____. At the maturity of the notes, Company A must pay $_____ and Company B

must pay $_____ to the lender.

Multiple Choice

Choose the best answer for each of the following questions and enter the identifying letter in the space provided.

_____ **1** When an allowance for the estimating of uncollectible accounts is in use, the writing off of an individual account receivable as worthless will:

a Be recorded by a debit to Uncollectible Accounts Expense.

b Increase the balance in the allowance account.

c Decrease the debit balance in the allowance account.

d Have no effect on the working capital of the company.

_____ **2** Bryan Company after aging its accounts receivable, estimated that $3,500 of the $125,000 of receivables on hand would probably prove uncollectible. The Allowance for Uncollectible Accounts contained a credit balance of $2,300 prior to adjustments. The appropriate accounting entry is:

a A debit to Uncollectible Accounts Expense and a credit to Allowance for Uncollectible Accounts for $1,200.

b A debit to Uncollectible Accounts Expense and a credit to Allowance for Uncollectible Accounts for $3,500.

c A debit to Uncollectible Accounts Expense and a credit to Allowance for Uncollectible Accounts for $5,800.

d A debit to Allowance for Uncollectible Accounts and a credit to Accounts Receivable for $3,500.

_____ **3** Pine Company uses the income statement approach in estimating uncollectible accounts expense and has found that such expense has consistently approximated 1% of net sales. At December 31 of the current year receivables total $50,000 and the Allowance for Uncollectible Accounts has a credit balance of $400 prior to adjustment. Net sales for the current year were $600,000. The adjusting entry should be:

a A debit to Uncollectible Accounts Expense and a credit to Allowance for Uncollectible Accounts for $5,600.

b A debit to Uncollectible Accounts Expense and a

credit to Allowance for Uncollectible Accounts for $6,400.

c A debit to Allowance for Uncollectible Accounts and a credit to Accounts Receivable for $6,000.

d A debit to Uncollectible Accounts Expense and a credit to Allowance for Uncollectible Accounts for $6,000.

_____ **4** The presence of the account Discount on Notes Payable indicates that:

a Money was borrowed on a short-term basis at a rate in excess of the going market rate.

b Assets were increased at the time of borrowing by an amount in excess of the cash received.

c Interest has been paid in advance of the due date.

d A note payable has been issued for an amount equal to the sum of the principal and interest payable on the maturity date of the note.

_____ **5** In contrasting the installment basis of recognizing revenue from installment sales with the method of recognizing revenue from a sale in the period in which the sale occurs, we can say that:

a Some concerns use the installment basis for income tax purposes, but not in their annual financial statements.

b The installment basis is widely used in published financial statements but is not permitted for income tax purposes.

c Accounting theory gives stronger support to the installment basis of accounting for installment sales.

d The installment basis is more complicated to apply but is more effective in the matching of revenue with related expenses.

_____ **6** The presence of the account Discount on Notes Receivable indicates that:

a A contingent liability exists.

b The face amount of a note receivable includes the interest receivable at the maturity date.

c Interest expense will be incurred in future periods.

d Total liabilities are less than if the discount had not been recorded.

_____ **7** Mann Company accepts numerous notes receivable from its customers. When the maker of a note defaults, Mann Company should:

a Transfer the principal of the note to Accounts Receivable and write off the accrued interest as a loss.

b Make no accounting entry if the maker of the defaulted note will sign a renewal note on equally favorable terms.

c Debit Accounts Receivable for the principal of the note plus interest earned, offset by credits to Notes Receivable and Interest Earned.

d Record a contingent liability for the maturity value of the note.

_____ **8** The term *imputing* interest means:

a Defaulting on the interest portion of a note payable.

b Recognizing interest revenue or expense on a cash basis.

c Treating a portion of the face amount of a note as interest.

d Providing an allowance for uncollectible interest on notes receivable.

Exercises

1 A list of account titles, each preceded by a code letter, appears below. Using this code, indicate the accounts to be debited and credited in properly recording the ten transactions described. In some cases more than one account may be debited or credited. (Note that **X designates any account not specified in the list.**)

A Cash
B Notes Receivable
C Accounts Receivable
D Allowance for Uncollectible Accounts
E Notes Payable
F Discount on Notes Payable
G Accrued Interest Payable
H Uncollectible Accounts Expense
I Interest Expense
J Credit Card Discount Expense
X Any account not listed

Transactions	Account(s) Debited	Account(s) Credited
Example: Sold merchandise, receiving part cash and the balance on account.	A, C	X
1 Wrote off the account of J. Smith as uncollectible.	H D	D
2 Borrowed $5,000 from a bank, signing a note for amount of $5,000, with interest stated at 8%.	a I	E
3 Collected cash from a national credit card company for credit card sales made this week.	a J	C
4 Discounted at bank a non-interest-bearing note receivable on same day note was received.	a F	X
5 Reinstated the account of J. Smith, written off in **1** above, when Smith promised to make payment.	D C	H D
6 Recognized interest expense for the period relating to $5,000 note payable. Note not yet due.	I	G
7 Borrowed from a bank, signing a note in which the face amount included the interest.	a F	E
8 Collected the J. Smith account in full.	a	B
9 Paid the $5,000 note originating in **2** above and all interest due, 20 days after making the adjusting entry in **6** above.	G E	a I
10 Recognized interest expense for the period relating to note originating in **7** above. Note not yet due.	F	G

2 Compute the interest on the following amounts by the 60-day, 6% method:

a $12,450 at 6% for 60 days: $_____

b $ 8,400 at 6% for 90 days: $_____

c $ 4,000 at 9% for 90 days: $_____

d $ 9,000 at 4% for 120 days: $_____

e $13,000 at 8% for 45 days: $_____

ELEVEN

INVENTORIES

HIGHLIGHTS OF THE CHAPTER

1 In previous chapters you have become familiar with the use of a dollar amount for inventory in both the balance sheet and the income statement; however, the amount for inventory has been given without much discussion as to its source.

2 In this chapter we consider what goods are properly included in inventory, how the quantity and the cost of the ending inventory are computed, and the advantages and disadvantages of several alternative methods of valuing inventory.

3 In a retail or wholesale business, inventory consists of **all goods owned and held for sale** in the regular course of business.

4 The **cost of goods available for sale** minus the **ending inventory** equals the **cost of goods sold.** When we assign a value to the ending inventory, we are thereby also determining the **cost of goods sold** and therefore the **gross profit on sales.**

5 The ending inventory of one year is the beginning inventory of the next year. Therefore an error in the valuation of ending inventory will cause the income statements of two successive years to be in error by the full amount of the error in inventory valuation.

6 a When **ending** inventory is understated, net income will be understated.

b When **ending** inventory is overstated, net income will be overstated.

c When **beginning** inventory is understated, net income will be overstated.

d When **beginning** inventory is overstated, net income will be understated.

7 In other words, an inventory error is **counterbalancing** over a two-year period. If ending inventory is overstated, the income for the current year will be overstated, but income for the following year will be understated by the same amount. The reverse is also true: if ending inventory is understated, the income for the current year will be understated but income for the following year will be overstated.

8 An error in inventory valuation will cause several parts of the financial statements to be in error. On the income statement, the cost of goods sold, the gross profit on sales, and the net income (before income taxes) will all be wrong by the full amount of the inventory error. On the balance sheet of the year in which the inventory error occurs, the owners' equity, the total current assets, and the balance sheet totals will also be in error.

9 Since an error in inventory has a counterbalancing effect on income over a two-year period, the owners' equity and the balance sheet totals will be correct at the end of the second year.

10 Taking a physical inventory is common practice at the end of each year. This means counting the merchandise owned, multiplying the quantity of each item by the unit cost to get a dollar value, and adding these values together to arrive at a total dollar figure for inventory.

11 Inventory includes all goods owned regardless of location. Title passes from seller to buyer when delivery is made. For goods in transit at year-end, we must consider the terms of shipment. If the terms of shipment are **F.O.B. shipping point,** the goods in transit are the property of the buyer. If the terms are **F.O.B. destination,** the goods remain the property of the seller while in transit.

12 The primary basis of accounting for inventory is **cost,** which includes transportation-in (the cost incurred in bringing the merchandise to the point where it is to be offered for sale).

13 When several lots of identical merchandise are purchased at different prices during the year, which price should be considered as the cost of the units remaining in the year-end inventory? We shall consider four alternative valuation methods: (a) specific identification, (b) average cost, (c) first-in, first-out, and (d) last-in, first-out.

14 The specific identification method **may** be used if the units in the ending inventory can be identified as having come from specific purchases.

15 The average-cost method is computed by dividing the total **cost** of units available for sale by the number of units available for sale. This **weighted average unit cost** is then multiplied by the number of units in the ending inventory.

16 The first-in, first-out method (**fifo**) is based on the assumption that the first merchandise acquired is the first sold. Therefore, ending inventory consists of the most recently acquired goods and is valued at the prices paid in the more recent purchases.

17 The last-in, first-out method (*lifo*) assumes that the most recently acquired goods are sold first, and that the ending inventory consists of the "old" merchandise acquired in the earliest purchases. Thus, the prices applied in valuing the ending inventory are the prices paid on the earliest purchases. The more recent prices are considered to apply to the cost of the goods sold.

18 During a period of changing prices, each of these four alternative inventory methods will lead to different figures for cost of goods, gross profit on sales, net income, and owners' equity. However, all are acceptable because they are merely alternative methods of measuring *cost.*

19 During a period of rising prices, the *lifo* method will lead to the smallest inventory value, the lowest net income, and the lowest income tax. This is because the more recent (and higher) costs are considered as being the cost of the units sold, and the earlier (and lower) purchase prices are considered to be the cost of the unsold units comprising the ending inventory. Supporters of lifo argue that income is most accurately measured by *matching* the *current* cost of merchandise against *current* sales prices regardless of which physical units of merchandise are actually delivered to customers.

20 The *fifo* method produces a realistic balance sheet amount for inventory close to current replacement cost, whereas the *lifo* method produces a balance sheet value for inventory reflecting prices in the distant past. On the other hand, lifo produces a more realistic income statement than does fifo because more current costs are deducted from revenue.

21 In a period of rising prices, the cost of replacing goods sold will exceed the historical cost of goods sold as reported in the income statement. Some accountants argue that the net income is therefore overstated since the business incurs a greater cost (the replacement cost) than is deducted from revenue (the historical cost) with respect to goods sold. The excess of the replacement cost of goods sold over their historical cost is termed *inventory profit.* Inventory profits are a restricted type of income, since inventory profits must be reinvested in inventory just to maintain inventory levels and therefore are not available to finance dividends or expansion or to pay income taxes.

22 In a period of rising prices, fifo produces a lower cost of goods sold than does lifo. Thus, the portion of net income which is "inventory profit" will be greater under fifo.

23 If the utility of inventory falls below cost because of deterioration, price level declines, or other reasons, it may be valued at the *lower of cost or market.* The word *market* in this context means *replacement* cost. The justification is prompt recognition of any loss which may have occurred. In no case should inventory be carried at more than its *net realizable value.*

24 The lower-of-cost-or-market rule may be applied to each item in the inventory, or to each category of inventory, or to the inventory as a whole.

25 The *gross profit method* of estimating inventories is useful when inventory is lost by fire or theft, or when it is desired to prepare monthly financial statements without incurring the expense of taking a physical inventory.

26 To apply the gross profit method, obtain from the ledger the figures for beginning inventory, purchases, and sales. Cost of goods sold is then computed by reducing the sales figure by the usual gross profit rate of prior periods. The difference between the cost of goods available for sale and the computed cost of goods sold represents the estimated ending inventory.

27 In retail stores, the merchandise is marked with the retail selling price. It is therefore convenient to use the *retail method of inventory,* which consists of pricing the inventory at selling price and then reducing it to cost by applying the ratio prevailing in the current period between cost and selling price. To use the retail method of inventory, it is necessary to maintain records of the beginning inventory and of the purchases in terms of selling price as well as of cost.

28 Whatever method of inventory valuation is selected, it should be followed consistently from period to period to avoid distorting reported income merely because of changes in accounting method.

29 In this chapter, we are primarily concerned with a *periodic inventory system* in which inventory is not known from day to day but is determined by taking a physical inventory periodically. The alternative is a *perpetual inventory system* which provides a continuous running balance of inventory. In using this system, purchases are debited to the Inventory account. A sale of merchandise requires two entries: (a) a debit to Cash (or Accounts Receivable) and a credit to Sales for the sales price and (b) a debit to Cost of Goods Sold and a credit to Inventory for the *cost* of the merchandise. Although more costly to operate, the perpetual inventory system is appropriate for a business dealing in goods of high unit value.

30 A manufacturing company has three inventories: raw materials, goods in process, and finished goods, all of which are classified as current assets on the balance sheet. The inventory of raw materials is priced in a manner similar to that used by a merchandising concern. The inventories of goods in process and finished goods are determined by estimating the cost incurred to produce the units on hand.

31 The difference in the income statement of a manufacturing company and that of a merchandising business lies in the *cost of goods sold* section. For a manufacturing company, *Cost of Finished Goods Manufactured* replaces the item labeled Purchases in the income statement of a merchandising business.

32 The amount appearing as Cost of Finished Goods Manufactured is determined from a financial statement entitled the *Statement of Cost of Finished Goods Manufactured.*

33 A statement of Cost of Finished Goods Manufactured begins with the cost of goods in process at the beginning of the period. To this amount the total *manufacturing costs* incurred during the period are added to give the total cost of goods in process during the period. This total is then allocated between the goods finished during the period and those which are still in process at the end of the period. The cost allocated to goods finished during the period is termed Cost of Finished Goods Manufactured and is used in the cost of goods sold section of the income statement.

TEST YOURSELF ON INVENTORIES

True or False

For each of the following statements, circle the T or the F to indicate whether the statement is true or false.

T F **1** A major objective of accounting for inventories is proper measurement of net income.

T F **2** An error in the valuation of inventory at the end of the period will cause errors in net income for two periods.

T F **3** Taking the inventory refers to the physical count to determine the quantity of inventory on hand; pricing the inventory means determining the cost of the inventory on hand.

T F **4** If the terms of shipment are F.O.B. shipping point, the goods in transit should normally belong to the seller.

T F **5** Errors in the valuation of inventory are counterbalancing; an error which causes an overstatement of net income this period will cause an understatement next period.

T F **6** Inventories are usually valued at cost, but the cost figure for an inventory can differ significantly depending upon what inventory method is used.

T F **7** The recording of a sale in the wrong period will have no effect on the net income for each period if the goods are excluded from inventory in the period in which the sale is recorded.

T F **8** An overstatement of ending inventory will cause an understatement of net income.

T F **9** The specific identification method of inventory valuation is particularly appropriate for low-priced, high-volume articles.

T F **10** The average-cost method places weight more on the prices at which large purchases were made than on the prices at which small purchases were made.

T F **11** Using the first-in, first-out (fifo) method during a period of rising prices implies that the cheaper goods have been sold and the more costly goods are still on hand.

T F **12** The last-in, first-out (lifo) method will give a lower dollar value for inventory than the fifo method if prices have been declining over the life of the business.

T F **13** During a period of rapid inflation, using lifo will maximize net income.

T F **14** Using the lifo method implies that the ending inventory consists of the most recently acquired goods.

T F **15** Inventory profits result from increasing the selling price of merchandise.

T F **16** The use of the lower-of-cost-or-market rule produces a conservative inventory valuation because unrealized losses are treated as actually incurred.

T F **17** The gross profit method permits a business to estimate ending inventory without actually taking a physical count of the goods on hand.

T F **18** The retail method of inventory valuation permits the physical inventory to be taken and priced at current retail prices rather than looking up invoices to determine the cost of goods on hand.

T F **19** Consistency in the valuation of inventories requires that a method once adopted cannot be changed unless the company is sold.

T F **20** A manufacturing business usually has three separate inventories: raw materials, manufacturing supplies, and finished goods.

T F **21** In the income statement of a manufacturing company. Cost of Finished Goods Manufactured replaces the item labeled Purchases in the income statement of a merchandising company.

T F **22** The cost of finished goods manufactured is equal to the beginning inventory of goods in process, plus total manufacturing costs, less the ending inventory of goods in process.

Completion Statements

Fill in the necessary words or amounts to complete the following statements:

1 If goods are shipped F.O.B. destination, the _____ to the goods while in transit belongs to the _____ and the goods should be excluded from the inventory of the _____.

2 Ending inventories are **overstated** as follows: Year 1 by $20,000; Year 2 by $8,000; and Year 3 by $15,000. Net income for each of the three years was computed at $25,000. The corrected net income figure (ignoring the effect of income taxes) for each of the three years is: Year 1, $_____; Year 2, $_____; Year 3, $_____.

3 The four most commonly used inventory valuation methods are: (a) _____ _____, (b) _____, (c) _____, and (d) _____.

4 During a period of inflation, the _____ method of inventory will maximize net income and give the (largest, smallest) _____ value for the asset inventory.

5 Inventory profits represent the difference between the historical cost of goods sold and the _____ _____ of goods sold. Inventory profits are a restricted type of income because they must be _____ in _____, and because they are not available to finance dividends or expansion. During a period of rising prices, companies using the _____ inventory method might be expected to have the largest inventory profits.

6 The lower-of-cost-or-market rule results in the recognition of a _____ in the _____ cost of inventory. However, an _____ in the _____ cost would not be recognized.

7 During a period of rising prices, using the _____ method implies that the cheaper goods are still on hand while the more expensive ones were sold.

8 The method of inventory valuation frequently used by retail stores is first to value the inventory at _____, and then to convert this amount to a _____ figure by applying the _____ of cost to selling prices during the current period.

9 The three inventory accounts of a manufacturing concern are: (a) _____ _____, (b) _____ _____ _____, and (c) _____.

10 Given below is certain information for a manufacturing concern:

Cost of raw materials used.	$ 80,000
Direct labor.	200,000
Total manufacturing cost incurred.	400,000
Total cost of goods in process during the year.	450,000
Good in process inventory, end of year. . . .	20,000
Decrease in finished goods inventory during the year.	7,500

From the information given above, complete the following:

(a) Goods in process inventory, beginning of year
$_____

(b) Factory overhead for the year: $_____

(c) Cost of finished goods manufactured: $_____.

(d) Cost of goods sold: $_____

Multiple Choice

Choose the best answer for each of the following questions and enter the identifying letter in the space provided.

_____ **1** One of the following is **not** an acceptable inventory method:
a Lower of cost or market.
b Sales value.
c Specific identification.
d First-in, first-out.

_____ **2** One of the following items would **not** be included in inventories on the balance sheet:

a Raw materials used in manufacture of chemicals.

b Raw materials on hand but not yet paid for.

c Cars left by customers with auto repair shop.

d Goods purchased but not yet delivered to premises (title passed).

_____ **3** An overstatement of $1,000 in the inventory at the end of Year 4 would:

a Understate the beginning inventory of Year 5.

b Have no effect on net income of Year 3.

c Overstate purchases for Year 5.

d Have no effect on net income of Year 4.

_____ **4** During a period of rising prices, which inventory pricing method might be expected to give the lowest valuation for inventory on the balance sheet and the lowest net income figure?

a Cost on a lifo basis.

b Cost on a fifo basis.

c Weighted average cost.

d Fifo, lower of cost or market.

_____ **5** The gross profit method of estimating inventories:

a Provides information about the number of units in the ending inventory.

b Provides information about changes in the rate of gross profit.

c Is a useful means of determining the rate of gross profit without taking a physical inventory.

d Is a useful means of verifying the reasonableness of a physical inventory count.

_____ **6** Goods costing $750 are sold for $1,000 at the end of Year 1, but the sale is recorded in Year 2. The goods **were** included in the ending inventory at the end of Year 1. The most likely effect of this error is:

a Net income for Year 1 was understated by $1,000.

b Net income for Year 2 was overstated by $250.

c Beginning inventory for Year 2 is understated by $750.

d Net income for Year 1 was overstated by $250.

_____ **7** The cost of finished goods manufactured is similar to one of the following items appearing in financial statements of a trading company:

a Cost of goods sold.

b Purchases (net of returns and allowances).

c Current assets.

d Merchandise inventory.

_____ **8** The cost of finished goods manufactured is computed by:

a Adding ending inventory of goods in process, raw materials used, direct labor, and factory overhead; subtracting beginning inventory of goods in process.

b Adding beginning inventory of goods in process, raw materials purchased, direct labor, and factory overhead; subtracting ending inventory of goods in process.

c Adding beginning inventory of goods in process, raw materials used, direct labor, and factory overhead; subtracting ending inventory of goods in process.

d Adding beginning inventory of finished goods, raw materials used, direct labor, and factory overhead; subtracting ending inventory of finished goods.

Exercises

1 The following inventory information is available for the month of May:

	Units	Total Cost
Beginning inventory, May 1..........	500	$5,000
Purchase, May 3..................	400	4,400
Purchase, May 10.................	800	9,600
Purchase, May 21.................	300	3,900

The replacement cost of each unit on May 31 is $12.50. Sales amounted to 1,500 units at an average price of $16.10.

Compute the cost of the ending inventory of 500 units and the cost of goods sold under each of the following inventory methods:

	Inventory	Cost of Goods Sold
a Fifo—cost..............	$_____	$_____
b Fifo—cost or market, whichever is lower............	$_____	$_____
c Lifo—cost..............	$_____	$_____
d Average—cost..........	$_____	$_____

2 On July 20, 19__, the accountant for B Company is in the process of preparing financial statements for the year ending June 30, 19__. The physical inventory, however, was not taken until July 10, 19__, and he finds it necessary to establish the approximate inventory cost at June 30, 19—, from the following data:

Physical inventory, July 10, 19— $30,000

Transactions for period July 1 to July 10:

Sales................................ 15,200

Sales returns........................ 400

Purchases........................... 17,500

Purchases returns.................... 550

The gross profit on sales of the past couple of years has averaged 22.5% of net sales.

In the space below, compute the approximate inventory cost at June 30, 19—.

3 Selected operating data as reported by the Chalet Company are presented below:

	Year 3	Year 2	Year 1
Beginning inventory.	$ 50,000	$ 45,000	$ 30,000
Ending inventory...	60,000	50,000	45,000
Purchases.........	400,000	380,000	375,000
Gross profit on sales	150,000	135,000	140,000
Net income........	80,000	60,000	20,000

An analysis of financial records discloses the following:

a A sale for $4,000 made on December 30 of Year 1 was not recorded until January 4 of Year 2. The cost of these goods, $3,200, was not included in the ending inventory at the end of Year 1.

b A purchase for $7,500 made on December 28 of Year 3 was not recorded until January 2 of Year 4. The goods were included in the inventory at the end of Year 3.

c The inventory count at the end of Year 2 was overstated by $10,000.

In the partially completed schedule below, prepare a corrected comparative income statement for the three-year period. Ignore income taxes.

CHALET COMPANY
Comparative Income Statement
For Years 1, 2, and 3

	Year 3	Year 2	Year 1
Sales.........................	$ 540,000	$ 510000	$ 500000
Cost of goods sold:			
Beginning inventory............	$ 50000	$ 45,000	$ 30,000
Purchases...................	392500	380,000	375,000
Cost of goods available for sale...	$ 442500	$ 425,000	$ 405,000
Less: Ending inventory..........	60,000	50000	45,000
Cost of goods sold........	$ 382500	$ 375000	$ 360,000
Gross profit on sales.................	$ 158000	$ 135000	$ 140000
Expenses.........................	70000	76000	120000
Net income......................	$ 82,500	$ 60000	$ 70000

Suggestion: Compute the expenses by deducting the net income as reported for each year from the gross profit on sales as reported for that year. Compute sales by adding the cost of goods sold to the gross profit on sales.

TWELVE

PLANT AND EQUIPMENT DEPRECIATION NATURAL RESOURCES AND INTANGIBLES

HIGHLIGHTS OF THE CHAPTER

1 The term **plant and equipment** is used to describe long-lived assets used in the operation of the business and not held for sale to customers. The term **fixed assets** has been used to describe plant assets but is now used less frequently.

2 A plant asset is a **bundle of services** to be received by the owner over a long period of time. As the services are received, a portion of the bundle (an asset) is consumed and is recognized as an expense (depreciation).

3 The major categories of plant and equipment include:

a Tangible plant assets, such as land, buildings, and machinery. Most of these assets are **subject to depreciation,** whereas land, for example, is generally **not subject to depreciation.**

b Intangible assets, such as patents, copyrights, trademarks, franchises, organization costs, leaseholds, and goodwill. Intangible assets can also be classified into (1) those with a limited term of existence and thus subject to **amortization** and (2) those with an unlimited term of existence and thus not subject to amortization.

4 The major accounting problems relating to plant and equipment are:

a Determining the cost of the plant asset.

b Procedures for allocating the cost of a plant asset to accounting periods.

c Recording costs (such as repairs) incurred in using plant assets.

d Recording the disposal of plant assets.

5 All **reasonable** and **necessary** expenditures incurred in acquiring a plant asset and placing it in use should be recorded in an asset account. The cost may include the list price, sales or use taxes paid, freight and handling costs, installation costs, and insurance prior to the time that the asset is placed in service.

6 Cash discounts reduce the net cost of the asset. Interest paid when an asset is purchased on the installment plan should be recorded as an expense rather than as part of the cost of acquiring the asset.

7 The cost of land may include real estate commissions, escrow fees, title insurance fees, delinquent taxes (including penalties and interest), etc. **Special assessments** for street paving or other improvements should be added to the cost of the land. Separate ledger accounts are always maintained for land and buildings. Certain land-improvement costs, such as fences, driveways, parking lots, sprinkler systems, and landscaping, have a limited life and should be recorded in a separate account and depreciated.

8 When a building is purchased, the total cost includes the price paid plus all incidental costs, such as termite inspection fees, legal fees, and major repairs necessary before the building is occupied. When a building is constructed by the owner, the total cost of the building includes all direct expenditures (labor, materials, building permit, etc.) plus a reasonable estimate of indirect costs (overhead).

9 *Depreciation* is the process of *allocating the cost of plant assets* to the periods in which services are received from the asset. A separate depreciation expense account should be maintained for each major group of depreciable assets, and the total amount of depreciation expense for the fiscal period should be disclosed in the income statement.

10 Depreciation is *not* a process of assigning a market value (or realizable value) to plant assets, nor is it a process of accumulating a fund for the replacement of assets when they become worn out or obsolete. Depreciation is an *allocation process:* the cost of an asset, less residual value, is allocated to the years that benefit from the use of the asset.

11 The two major causes of depreciation are:
a Physical deterioration from use.
b Obsolescence due to technological changes or changing needs of the company.

12 The methods of computing periodic depreciation are:
a Straight-line:

$$\frac{\text{Cost} - \text{residual value}}{\text{Estimated years of useful life}}$$

b Units of output:

$$\frac{\text{Cost} - \text{residual value}}{\text{Total estimated units of output}} \times \text{units produced}$$

c Fixed-percentage-on-declining-balance: Book value of asset multiplied by a rate which is usually twice the straight-line rate.
d Sum-of-the-years'-digits: Cost minus residual value multiplied by a fraction, of which the numerator is the remaining years of useful life and the denominator is the sum of the years of useful life.

13 The *straight-line method* is the simplest and the most widely used method of computing depreciation. Under this method an *equal portion* of the cost of the asset (less residual value) is allocated to each period of use. This method is most appropriate when usage of an asset is fairly uniform from period to period.

14 When the usage of an asset fluctuates and output can be estimated in terms of some unit (such as tons produced or miles driven), a more equitable allocation of a plant asset can be obtained by computing depreciation on the basis of output. Cost (less residual value) is divided by estimated output to obtain a depreciation *rate per unit.* Depreciation for a period is computed by multiplying the rate per unit by the number of units produced.

15 Under *accelerated depreciation* methods, larger amounts of depreciation are recorded in the early years of use and reduced amounts in later years. Accelerated methods are particularly appropriate when obsolescence is more significant than physical deterioration in rendering the asset less useful or productive. In some cases the use of an accelerated depreciation method tends to equalize the total expense of using an asset because decreasing periodic depreciation charges are offset by increasing repair outlays as the asset gets older.

16 The chief advantage of accelerated depreciation lies in the fact that its use for income tax purposes reduces taxable income in the early years of an asset's life and reduces the amount of taxes paid, thereby making more funds available for use in the business.

17 A business need not use the same method of depreciation for all its assets. Also, different methods may be used for tax purposes than are being used in the accounting records and financial statements.

18 Depreciation rates are based on estimates of useful life. If the estimate of useful service life is found to be in error, the estimate should be revised, and the *undepreciated cost of the asset should be allocated over the years of remaining useful life.* A change in annual depreciation expense may also result from a change in the *estimate of residual value* or from a change in the *method* of computing depreciation.

19 A *capital expenditure* is one that will benefit many accounting periods; a *revenue expenditure* is one that will benefit only the current accounting period. Capital expenditures are recorded in asset accounts and are deducted from revenue through the process of depreciation; revenue expenditures are recorded in expense accounts as incurred.

20 When units of plant and equipment wear out or become obsolete they must be discarded, sold, or traded in. To record the disposal of a depreciable asset, the cost of the asset must be removed from the asset account, *and the accumulated depreciation* (on that asset) *must be removed* from the contra-asset account.

21 The *book value,* or carrying value, of a depreciable asset is its cost minus accumulated depreciation. If the asset is sold for a price above book value, there is a *gain* on the sale. If the asset is sold for less than book value, there is a *loss.*

22 No gain or loss is recognized when a depreciable asset is *traded in* on a similar asset. The cost of the new asset is recorded as the sum of the *book value of the old asset plus any additional amount paid* (or to be paid) for the new asset.

23 Natural resources, such as mines or standing

timber, are physically extracted and converted into inventory. These assets are recorded at cost and reported separately in the balance sheet.

24 **Depletion** is the process of **allocating the cost** of a natural resource to the units removed. The depletion rate is computed by dividing the cost of the natural resource by the estimated number of units available to be removed. The rate is then multiplied by the number of units removed during a period to determine the total depletion charge for the period.

25 **Intangible assets** are those noncurrent assets which do not have physical substance but contribute to the revenue of the business. Intangibles are recorded at cost, and should be **amortized** over the periods of their usefulness. The amortization of goodwill is not permitted for income tax purposes, but is required in the preparation of financial statements.

26 **Goodwill** is the market value of a going business **in excess of** the fair market value of the other identifiable assets of the business. It represents the present value of expected future earnings above the earnings normally realized in the industry.

27 Goodwill may exist in many businesses, but it should be recorded in the accounts **only when it is purchased.**

28 The following three methods may be used in **estimating** the value of goodwill owned by a business unit:

a Negotiated agreement between buyer and seller. If a business with net assets (at market value) of $80,000 is sold for $100,000, this suggests that goodwill of $20,000 is identified with this business.

b A multiple of the amount by which the average annual earnings exceed normal earnings. If the normal earnings are estimated at $20,000 and average annual earnings are $22,500, goodwill may be estimated at, say, five times excess earnings ($22,500 − $20,000), or $12,500.

c The capitalized value of excess earning power. For example, if excess earnings amount to $5,000 and the capitalization rate agreed upon is 20%, the goodwill would be estimated at $25,000 ($5,000 ÷ .20 = $25,000).

TEST YOURSELF ON
PLANT AND EQUIPMENT; DEPRECIATION

True or False

For each of the following statements, circle the T or the F to indicate whether the statement is true or false.

T F 1 In a broad sense, the cost of a machine or a building may be viewed as a long-term prepaid expense.

T F 2 An auto owned by a glass manufacturer would be reported under Plant and Equipment, while glass owned by an auto manufacturer would be classified as Inventory.

T F 3 Land improvements, like land, should not be depreciated since they have an unlimited life.

T F 4 Obsolescence may be a more significant factor than wear and tear through use in putting an end to the usefulness of many depreciable assets.

T F 5 Depreciation expense for a period should be a reasonably good estimate of the reduction in the fair market value of an asset during the period.

T F 6 If the price of construction goes up by 25% during Year 1, the amount of depreciation on a building already owned will be increased, but not necessarily by 25%.

T F 7 In practice, the residual value of an asset is often ignored in estimating annual depreciation expense.

T F 8 The units-of-output method of depreciation yields similar results to **accelerated** methods of depreciation when the rate of output increases steadily over a period of years.

T F 9 The Accumulated Depreciation account is a fund established for the replacement of assets, but it will not be large enough to cover the cost of replacement during a period of inflation.

T F 10 The sum-of-the-years'-digits method and the units-of-output method are called accelerated depreciation methods.

T F 11 The fixed-percentage-on-declining-balance method of depreciation has a "built-in" residual value and can never allocate 100% of the original cost of an asset to expense.

T F 12 If accelerated depreciation is used for tax purposes, it must also be used for financial reporting purposes.

T F 13 When it becomes evident that a plant asset will have a useful life longer than had been originally estimated, the depreciation rate will be revised according to the new estimate of useful life.

T F 14 **Capital expenditures** are those disbursements which are allocated to several accounting periods; **revenue expenditures** are charged off as current expenses.

T F 15 Whenever a depreciable asset is sold, both the cost of the asset and the accumulated depreciation must be removed from the accounts.

T F 16 For tax purposes a gain is recognized when the trade-in allowance on an asset exceeds its book value.

T F 17 When an asset is traded in on a similar asset and the transaction is recorded in a manner acceptable for tax purposes, the cost recorded for the new asset will be the book value of the old asset plus any amount paid in addition to trading in the old asset.

T F 18 Depletion refers to the allocation of the cost of an intangible asset over the periods that benefits are received.

T F 19 Intangible assets are assets that cannot be sold.

T F 20 Often, intangible assets are written off to expense immediately because determining the periods in which benefits will be received may be nearly impossible.

T F 21 The systematic write-off of intangible assets to expense is known as amortization.

T F 22 Goodwill is the present value of future earnings in excess of the earnings normally realized in an industry.

T F 23 When a business has superior earnings for many years, goodwill probably exists and should be recorded in the accounts.

T F 24 If a buyer of a business pays a price for the business in excess of the fair market value of the net tangible assets, he may record goodwill as one of the assets he is acquiring.

Completion Statements

Fill in the necessary words or amounts to complete the following statements:

1 The two causes of depreciation are: (a) _____ _____ and (b) _____.

2 If a _____ expenditure is erroneously recorded as a _____ expenditure, net income will be _____ in the current period, and overstated in every future period in which depreciation should have been recognized.

3 Net income for three consecutive years was reported as follows:

Year 1 . . . . $30,000
Year 2 . . . . $39,000
Year 3 . . . . $40,000

At the beginning of Year 1 a capital expenditure of $15,000 for a new machine, which should have been depreciated over a five-year life using the sum-of-the-years'-digits method, was erroneously

charged to repair expense. The correct net income for the three years should have been as follows:

Year 1, $_____; Year 2, $_____; Year 3, $_____.

4 Extraordinary repairs are repairs that _____ the _____ _____ of a plant asset beyond the original estimate. An extraordinary repair on a delivery truck would be recorded as a debit to the _____ _____ account.

5 The entry to record the disposal of a depreciable asset will always include a credit to the asset account for the _____ _____ of the asset, and a debit to the _____ _____ account.

6 Tax regulations provide that the cost of new equipment shall be the sum of the _____ _____ of any old equipment traded in plus any _____ _____ paid or to be paid in acquiring the new equipment.

7 Intangible assets are assets that lack _____ _____ and do not qualify for inclusion in the _____ _____ section of the balance sheet. The cost of these assets is allocated over their useful lives through the process of _____ _____.

8 Goodwill is the _____ _____ of estimated future earnings in _____ of earnings normally realized in an industry. Goodwill is recorded in the accounts only when it is _____ _____.

Multiple Choice

Choose the best answer for each of the following questions and enter the identifying letter in the space provided.

_____ **1** Big Company purchased land for $80,000 subject to delinquent property taxes of $4,000. These taxes were paid immediately by Big Company along with interest of $320 on the delinquent taxes. The cost of this land should be recorded by Big Company at:
a $80,000
b $84,000
c $84,320
d Some other amount.

_____ **2** The book value or carrying value of a depreciable asset is best defined as:

a The undepreciated cost of the asset.

b The price that the asset would bring if offered for sale.

c Accumulated depreciation on the asset since acquisition.

d Original cost of the asset.

_____ *3* The straight-line method of depreciation:

a Generally gives best results because it is easy to apply.

b Ignores fluctuations in the rate of asset usage.

c Should be used in a period of inflation because it accumulates, at a uniform rate, the fund for the replacement of the asset.

d Is the best method to use for income tax purposes.

_____ *4 Accumulated depreciation,* as used in accounting, may be defined as:

a Earnings retained in the business that will be used to purchase another asset when the present asset is depreciated.

b Funds (or cash) set aside to replace the asset being depreciated.

c The portion of the cost of a plant asset recognized as expense since the asset was acquired.

d An expense of doing business.

_____ *5* A and B Companies purchase identical equipment having an estimated service life of 10 years. A Company uses the straight-line method of depreciation, and B Company uses the sum-of-the-years'-digits method. Assuming that the companies are identical in all other respects:

a B Company will record more depreciation on this asset over the entire 10 years than will A Company.

b At the end of the third year, the book value of the asset will be lower on A Company's books than on B Company's.

c A Company's depreciation expense will be greater in the first year than B Company's.

d A Company's net income will be lower in the ninth year than B Company's.

_____ *6* Which of the following is not an intangible asset?

a A patent.

b A copyright.

c An investment in common stock.

d Goodwill.

_____ *7* The best evidence of goodwill existing in a business is:

a The appearance of goodwill on the balance sheet.

b Numerous contributions to charitable organizations.

c A long-standing reputation for manufacturing a high-quality product.

d A long record of earnings greater than those of like-size firms in the same industry.

_____ *8* Lucky Strike Mines recognizes $2 of deple-tion for each ton of ore mined. This year 750,000 tons of ore were mined, but only 700,000 tons were sold. The amount of depletion that should be deducted from revenue this year is:

a $2,900,000

b $1,500,000

c $1,400,000

d $100,000

_____ *9* X Company has traded in a machine on a similar asset, paying cash for the difference between list price and the trade-in allowance. Generally, accountants would record the new asset on the books at:

a The list price of the new asset.

b The estimated fair value of the old asset plus the cash paid.

c The book value of the old asset plus the cash paid.

d The trade-in allowance on the old asset plus the cash paid.

Exercises

1 A truck with an estimated life of four years was acquired on March 31, Year 1, for $11,000. The estimated residual value of the truck is $1,000, and the service life is estimated at 100,000 miles. Compute depreciation for Year 1 and Year 2, using the following methods:

	Year 1	Year 2
a Straight-line	$_____	$_____
b Output (miles driven: Year 1, 20,000; Year 2, 40,000)	$_____	$_____
c Sum-of-the-years'-digits . .	$_____	$_____
d Fixed-percentage-on-declining-balance (twice the straight-line rate)	$_____	$_____

2 A machine which cost $6,000 had an estimated useful life of six years and an estimated salvage value of $600. Straight-line depreciation was used. In the space on page 76, prepare the journal entry (omitting explanation) to record the disposal of the machine under each of the following assumptions:

a The machine was sold for $4,000 cash after two years' use.

b After three years' use, the machine was sold for $3,500 cash.

c After four years' use, the machine was traded in on a similar machine with a list price of $8,000. The trade-in allowance was $3,100. (Record in a manner acceptable for income tax purposes.)

	General Journal		
a			
b			
c			

3 The Golden Calf, a Las Vegas gambling casino, had net tangible assets of $4,000,000 and earned an average net income of $1,040,000 per year. Other Las Vegas casinos averaged a net income equal to 20% of their net tangible assets. An investment group negotiating to buy the Golden Calf offers to pay $4,000,000 for the casino's net tangible assets, plus an amount for goodwill.

The investment group determined the amount to be paid for goodwill by capitalizing the Golden Calf's annual earnings in excess of the industry average earnings at a rate of 25%. Compute the total price the investment group is offering to pay for the Golden Calf.

Computations:

Answer: $_____

THIRTEEN

BONDS PAYABLE LEASES AND OTHER LIABILITIES

HIGHLIGHTS OF THE CHAPTER

1 Raising capital to meet business needs is one of the more important and more difficult functions of management. Funds to meet seasonal needs are generally provided through bank borrowing and the expansion of accounts payable; long-term needs may be provided through the retention of earnings, and also through the issuance of bonds, long-term notes, and capital stock, or the retention of earnings.

2 **Bonds payable** are a popular form of long-term financing. Bonds payable may be secured by specific property or may be unsecured. An unsecured bond is referred to as a **debenture bond.** Most bonds have a single maturity date (for example, 20 or 25 years from date of issue); some bond issues provide for varying maturity dates and are known as **serial bonds.**

3 Most bonds are **callable** at the option of the issuing corporation at stipulated dates and prices. Bonds may be **convertible** into common stock at the option of the bondholder. Convertible bonds have the advantage of giving the issuer a deductible interest expense and the investor a fixed income until conversion. If the corporation is successful and the price of its common stock appreciates substantially, the bondholder can share in the company's success by converting his bonds into common stock.

4 Most bonds currently being issued are **registered** in contrast to **coupon** bonds which were popular some years ago. When a bond is registered, the owner of record receives the periodic interest checks; when bonds have coupons attached, the holder of the bonds receives periodic interest by presenting the appropriate coupon for payment.

5 Bonds of large and well-established companies are readily transferable because they are generally traded on one or more security exchanges. The quotations for bonds are usually given in terms of a percentage of the par value. Thus, a $1,000 bond at 101⅞ would bring $1,018.75, before deducting commissions or taking accrued interest into account.

6 The amount of bonds that a company should issue depends on the nature of the industry in which the company operates and the company's ability to utilize capital profitably. If a company, for example, can earn 10% on assets invested in the business, it would generally be advantageous to the common stockholders if the company would finance expansion through the issuance of, say, 8% bonds. If the company could earn only 6% on the money borrowed, it would not be profitable to issue 8% bonds. Issuing bonds to provide some of the capital needs is referred to as **trading on the equity.**

7 Bonds generally pay interest every six months. When bonds are issued between interest dates, the buyer is charged for the accrued interest to date of sale, and the issuing corporation credits Bond Interest Payable. This account is then debited (along with Bond Interest Expense) at the semiannual interest payment date.

8 If the contractual rate of interest that the bonds pay is lower than the going market rate, the **bonds will sell at a discount.** If the bonds pay a rate in excess of the going market rate, the **bonds will sell at a premium.** Any bond discount is deducted from the par value of the bonds and any premium is added to the par value in reporting bonds payable in the balance sheet.

9 In order to measure the actual interest expense on the books of the issuing corporation, the bond discount or premium must be **amortized over the remaining life of the bonds.** Amortization of bond discount results in an interest expense amount in excess of the interest actually paid in cash; amortization of premium reduces interest expense below the amount of interest paid in cash.

10 The **carrying value** of bonds payable is the par value of the bonds plus any unamortized premium or minus any unamortized discount. If bonds are retired before maturity at a price above carrying value, a loss results; if bonds are retired at a price below carrying value, a gain is realized.

11 Because the conversion feature of **convertible bonds** gives bondholders a potential opportunity to profit from a rise in the market price of the issuing company's common stock, convertible bonds generally carry a lower interest rate than nonconvertible bonds.

12 No gain or loss is recognized by the issuing corporation upon the conversion of bonds into common stock. The carrying value of the bonds converted is assigned to the common stock issued.

13 A **bond sinking fund** may be accumulated in order to have sufficient cash to pay off the liability when the bonds mature. The fund is accumulated through periodic deposits (usually with a trustee who invests the cash in income-yielding securities) and represents an asset (reported as an investment in the balance sheet) of the corporation.

14 Mortgages payable generally call for monthly payments, including interest and repayment of principal. The portion of unpaid principal maturing within one year should be classified as a current liability in the balance sheet.

15 A **lease** is a contract in which the **lessor** gives the **lessee** the right to use an asset in return for periodic rental payments. Leasing contracts may take the form of an **operating lease** in which the lessor retains the usual risks and rewards of ownership, or a **financing lease** in which the main objectives are to provide financing to the lessee and to transfer to the lessee the usual risks and rewards of ownership.

16 In an operating lease, the periodic rentals are recorded as revenue by the lessor and as rental expense by the lessee. No liability is recognized by the lessee other than for any unpaid monthly rentals.

17 A financing lease which **is considered equivalent to a sale and purchase** should be recorded as an installment sale of property by the lessor and as a purchase of property by the lessee. The asset and related liability should be recorded by the lessee at the **present value** of the future rental payments.

A financing lease which **is not** considered equivalent to a sale and purchase simply gives the lessee a **property right** in the leased asset.

18 Some accountants feel that the property rights resulting from certain types of financing leases should be **capitalized** by the lessee. Capitalization of such leases by a lessee would require the recognition of both an asset and a liability in the lessee's balance sheet.

19 Under a **funded pension plan,** accrued pension obligations are recorded by a debit to Pension Expense and a credit to Cash (or Liability under Pension Plan). When employees retire, the retirement benefits are paid by an insurance company or some other outside agency. In an **unfunded plan,** payments to retired employees are recorded as debits to Liability under Pension Plan and credits to Cash.

20 The most common accrued liabilities found in the balance sheets of many businesses relate to payrolls. These include FICA Tax Payable, Liability for Income Tax Withheld, Accrued Payroll, State Unemployment Tax Payable, and Federal Unemployment Tax Payable.

21 Deductions from the earnings of employees include: social security taxes, income tax withheld, and possibly unemployment taxes, union dues, insurance premiums, etc.

22 Payroll taxes on the employer include social security taxes, federal unemployment insurance tax, and state unemployment tax. Payroll taxes on the employer plus total salaries expense represent the total cost of labor services for a business enterprise.

23 A business must use the calendar year in accounting for payroll taxes. The employer must file payroll tax returns as follows:

a Income tax withheld and FICA taxes due—before the end of the month following each calendar quarter.

b Federal unemployment tax return—by January 31 for the preceding calendar year.

c State unemployment compensation returns—usually before the end of the month following each calendar quarter.

24 An **estimated liability** is an obligation known to exist, but for which **the dollar amount is uncertain;** a **contingent liability,** on the other hand, **may or may not exist,** depending on the outcome of some future event. Estimated liabilities usually appear among current liabilities in the balance sheet; contingent liabilities should be fully disclosed in the notes which accompany the financial statements.

TEST YOURSELF ON BONDS PAYABLE, LEASES, AND OTHER LIABILITIES

True or False

For each of the following statements, circle the T or the F to indicate whether the statement is true or false.

T F 1 A corporation will generally try to expand accounts payable and short-term bank borrowing in order to provide funds for plant expansion.

T F 2 Formal approval by the board of directors and by the stockholders is usually required before bonds are issued.

T F 3 Debenture bonds generally are not callable or convertible into common stock.

T F 4 Both the interest on bonds payable and dividends on capital stock are deductible in computing the taxable income for a corporation.

T F 5 Borrowing money to conduct business is known as trading on the equity.

T F 6 Authorized but unissued bonds payable should be included in the balance sheet as an asset since they represent a potential source of cash.

T F 7 When bonds are issued between interest dates, Bond Interest Expense should be debited for the interest accrued to date of issuance.

T F 8 Total interest expense on bonds sold for less than face value will be the cash paid as interest less the amortization of the discount for the period.

T F 9 When the rate of interest on the open market is 8%, a 9% bond will sell at a premium.

T F 10 Bonds sell at a discount when the coupon rate is larger than the going rate of interest.

T F 11 If a bond with a carrying value of $1,010 is retired by the issuing company at 104, a loss of $30 on the retirement of bonds will result.

T F 12 In accruing interest expense at the end of the period, the premium or discount on bonds payable should be amortized to the balance sheet date.

T F 13 A gain or loss should be recognized by the issuing corporation upon conversion of bonds into common stock.

T F 14 Securities held in a bond sinking fund are generally included under current assets in the balance sheet.

T F 15 Mortgages payable usually call for equal monthly payments, consisting of interest on the unpaid balance for one month and a partial repayment of the principal.

T F 16 Leases which contain provisions indicating that they are in effect equivalent to a sale and purchase of assets are called operating leases.

T F 17 A funded pension plan does not require the recognition of pension expense in the accounting records of the employer company.

T F 18 If a worker earns $20,000 a year and the FICA tax rate is 6%, the government will receive a total of $2,400 representing the employee's and employer's FICA contribution for the year.

T F 19 The employer, not the employee, is responsible for making proper payment to government agencies for income and social security taxes withheld.

T F 20 Estimated liabilities are those contingent liabilities which can be measured with reasonable certainty and which are relatively small in amount.

Completion Statements

Fill in the necessary words or amounts to complete the following statements:

1 If additional shares of stock are issued without a proportional increase in total net income, the earnings per share will (increase or decrease) _____.

2 If $1 million of bonds payable, which were issued at par, are called at 105, a (gain or loss) _____ of $_____ would result on the transaction.

3 As the discount on bonds payable is amortized, the amount of the net bond liability (increases or decreases) _____; as the premium on bonds payable is amortized, the amount of the net bond liability (increases or decreases) _____ _____.

4 Bonds are convertible into common stock at a conversion ratio of $20 for each share. The conversion of $2 million of bonds will require the issuance of _____ additional shares of common stock.

5 Examples of long-term liabilities, other than bonds payable, are: (a) _____ _____, (b) _____ _____ _____, (c) _____

6 The typical deductions from an employee's gross earnings include: (a) _____,

(b) _____

_____, (c) _____

_____

_____.

7 Payroll taxes levied on the employer usually consist of: (a) _____ _____, (b)

_____

_____, (c) _____

_____.

8 FICA taxes apply only on the first $_____

of earnings at the rate of _____% (as assumed in the text).

9 Form _____ is a withholding statement, furnished by the employer to employees and to the

_____.

10 Current liability accounts relating to payrolls are:

(a) _____,

(b) _____

_____, (c) _____

_____,

(d) _____.

Multiple Choice

Choose the best answer for each of the following questions and enter the identifying letter in the space provided.

_____ **1** A part of the balance in one of the following accounts may be reported as a current liability:
a Capital Stock Subscribed.
b Mortgage Note Payable.
c Bond Sinking Fund.
d Accrued Payroll.

_____ **2** One of the following is *not* a typical characteristic of bonds payable:
a Callable.
b Registered.
c Participating.
d Par value.

_____ **3** Convertible bonds issued by business enterprises:

a Are generally sold by companies with a weak financial position.
b Should not be issued if convertible preferred stock can be sold to investors.
c Are sold in order to sell the common stock at a better price (in effect) at the time of conversion and to offer investors an opportunity to share in the success of the issuing corporation.
d Should be reported in the stockholders' equity section of the balance sheet.

_____ **4** The discount on bonds payable is best described as:
a An element of interest expense on borrowed funds that will be paid by the issuing corporation at maturity.
b The payment of periodic interest at less than the rate called for in the bond contract.
c An amount below par which the bondholder may be called upon to make good.
d An asset representing interest that has been paid in advance.

_____ **5** The account Premium on Bonds Payable is best classified in the balance sheet as:
a An addition to bonds payable.
b An appropriation of retained earnings.
c A deduction from bonds payable.
d An asset.

_____ **6** Rex Corporation has been authorized to issue 8%, 20-year bonds payable. At the issue date the market rate of interest for this quality of bonds is 7.9%. On the basis of these facts, it might be expected that:
a The company will find it difficult to sell the bonds.
b The bonds will be issued at a premium.
c The bonds will be issued at a discount.
d The bond contract will be rewritten.

_____ **7** Convertible bonds:
a Are not popular among investors.
b Generally bear a rate of interest below the rate for similar nonconvertible bonds.
c Are convertible at the option of the issuing corporation.
d Should be classified as a current liability in the balance sheet if conversion is imminent.

_____ **8** State unemployment taxes are:
a Levied on employees at the rate of 2.7% of the first $4,200 of annual earnings by each employee.
b Levied on employees at rates which differ among the states.
c Levied on employers and represent an expense of doing business.

d Paid to the federal government and allocated to the various states as needed.

_____ *9* The earnings per share of the Simiar Company amount to $2.30 on 100,000 shares outstanding. If $1 million of 6% bonds are issued and the company earns 10% (before income taxes of 40%) on the additional funds, the earnings per share should increase to:

a $3.30
b $2.70
c $2.54
d Some other amount.

_____ *10* A sinking fund is established for the retirement of bonds by making equal annual deposits of $25,000 at the end of each year starting in Year 1. The balance on deposit is invested at the rate of 6%. The amount of the fund immediately after making the deposit at the end of Year 3 is:

a $75,000
b $78,000
c $51,500
d $79,590

Exercises

1 On July 1, 1976, Caldwell Co. issued $600,000 of 5%, 10-year bonds with interest payable on March 1 and September 1. The company received cash of $604,200, including the accrued interest from March 1, 1976. Place the correct answer to each of the following questions in the space provided. (Use the space provided for computations.)

a What was the amount of accrued interest on July 1, 1976? $_____ .

b What was the amount of bond discount or premium (state which) to be amortized over the period that the bonds will be outstanding, 116 months? $_____ .

c What was the amount of cash paid to bondholders on September 1, 1976? $_____ .

d What amount of accrued interest payable should appear on the balance sheet on December 31, 1976? $_____ .

e What was the amount of the unamortized discount or premium on December 31, 1976? $_____ .

f What was the total interest expense for 1976 relating to this bond issue? $_____ .

Computations

2 From the data in Exercise 1, prepare journal entries required on each of the following dates. (Use the space provided below.)

a July 1, 1976 (issuance of bonds).

b September 1, 1976 (payment of interest and amortization for two months).

c December 31, 1976 (accrual of interest and amortization from September 1 to December 31).

	1976	General Journal		
a	July 1			
b	Sept. 1			
c	Dec. 31			

3 The Ryan Corporation has a payroll for the month of January as follows:

Manufacturing wages.	$6,700
Sales salaries.	1,500
Administrative salaries.	1,800

FICA taxes are 6% of the first $13,200 earned by each employee. Federal unemployment taxes are 3.2% of wages up to $4,200 a year, but a credit against this tax is given for payment to the state of 2.7% of wages up to $4,200 a year. Federal income tax of $1,350 was withheld during January.

In the space provided below, prepare journal entries to record (a) the payroll for January, including withholding from employees, and (b) the employer's payroll taxes for January. (Use a single account to record the payroll taxes expense.)

	19____	General Journal		
a	Jan. 31			

b	Jan. 31			

4 You have been asked to assist the president of a newly organized company to prepare a plan to raise the $10 million in capital required to start operations. A committee of the board of directors has proposed the following three plans:

Plan A: Sell 1 million shares of common stock at $10.

Plan B: Sell 500,000 shares of common stock at $10 and 100,000 shares of 7%, $50 par preferred stock at $50 per share.

Plan C: Sell 500,000 shares of common stock at $10 and $5 million of 7% bonds at par.

The company expects to earn 8% on the $10 million investment in the first year of operations before paying interest on bonds (if any) and income taxes at the rate of 40%.

Prepare a statement showing earnings per share of common stock under each of the three proposals. Use the partially completed schedule below:

	Plan A (common stock only)	Plan B (common and preferred stock)	Plan C (common stock and bonds)
Earnings, before interest and income taxes	$	$	$
Less: Interest on bonds			
Earnings before income taxes	$	$	$
Income taxes, 40%			
Net income	$	$	$
Less: Dividend on preferred stock			
Net income available for common stock	$	$	$
Number of shares of common stock outstanding			
Net income per share of common stock	$	$	$

FOURTEEN

ACCOUNTING PRINCIPLES

HIGHLIGHTS OF THE CHAPTER

1 Modern corporations are usually managed by professional managers rather than by the owners. These managers are accountable to the owners, as well as to creditors, employees, and certain government agencies.

2 The primary means by which management reports to these outsiders is by periodic financial statements. These statements are used by interested parties to evaluate management's performance, to measure borrowing power, to guide investment decisions, and to formulate public policy.

3 To be useful, these statements must be clearly **understandable, reliable,** and also **comparable** so that users may evaluate the performance of one business relative to that of others. To achieve these objectives, some "ground rules" for financial reporting are necessary

4 **Generally accepted accounting principles** are the ground rules for financial reporting. The financial statements of all publicly owned corporations are prepared in conformity with these principles.

5 In order to qualify as "generally accepted," an accounting principle should be widely used and should be supported by one or more of the following groups:

a The **AICPA** (the professional association of licensed CPAs), through the pronouncements of the **Financial Accounting Standards Board** and its predecessor, the **Accounting Principles Board.**

b The **American Accounting Association** (an organization composed primarily of accounting professors), through research reports and monographs.

c The **Securities and Exchange Commission** (an agency of the federal government), through publication of **Accounting Series Releases.**

6 One basic accounting principle is that the information in an accounting report is compiled for a carefully defined **accounting entity.** An individual, a division of a corporation, or a whole business enterprise are all examples of possible accounting entities. The important thing is that the entity is clearly defined before the reports are prepared, and then only the activities of that entity are reported. If we prepare financial statements only for the Chevrolet Division of General Motors, we would not include the expenses incurred by the Pontiac Division. If the whole company of General Motors is to be the subject of the financial statements, the activities of all the General Motors' divisions should be included.

7 An accounting entity does not have to be a legal entity. For example, a corporation is a legal entity, whereas a single proprietorship is not. A **consolidated accounting** entity includes two or more legal corporate entities. Most large businesses are actually consolidated entities.

8 Another important principle is the **going-concern principle.** This means that we assume that a business will continue in operation for an indefinite period of time sufficient to carry out all of its commitments. The going-concern principle is the reason why all assets are not valued at their liquidating value.

9 The preparation of **periodic** financial reports is another accounting principle. To be useful, financial statements must be timely and available at frequent intervals so that decision makers may observe trends and changes in the economic condition of an accounting entity. However, when the life of a business is divided into specific **fiscal periods** (accounting periods), the results can only be estimates. For instance, the portion of the cost of a building to be deducted from the revenue of the current month is based upon an estimate of how long the building will be used.

10 Another principle underlying financial statements is the **stability of the measuring unit.** We assume that the dollar is constant and that it does not change in **purchasing power.** This means we ignore changes in the purchasing power of the dollar resulting from inflation or deflation. For example, since 1960 there has been inflation in the United States. A dollar will not buy as much today as it did in 1960. If we bought $15,000 worth of land in 1960, it might cost $30,000 or more to buy a similar piece of land today, just because of inflation. However, assets are not written up to current dollar values in financial statements: we make the simplifying assumption that the value of the dollar is constant and does not change over time.

11 *Objectivity* is one of the most basic accounting principles. This means that the valuation of assets and liabilities is based on *objective evidence,* such as an actual *exchange price.* An objective value is one that is free from *bias* and can be verified by an independent party. Objectivity is one reason why assets are valued at historical cost (an actual exchange price) rather than at estimated current market value.

12 Even though objectivity is a major goal of accounting, some measurements must still be estimates based on judgment. Depreciation, for example, is not completely objective because it depends upon an estimate of useful life.

13 Both the balance sheet and the income statement are affected by the *cost principle.* Assets are valued at their *cost,* rather than at their current market values. Expenses represent the *cost* of goods and services used up in the effort to generate revenue. The major argument supporting the cost principle is that cost can be determined *more objectively* than can current market value.

14 The timing of revenue recognition is determined by the *realization principle.* Accountants usually do not recognize revenue until it is realized. Revenue is realized when (a) the earning process is essentially complete, and (b) objective evidence exists as to the amount of revenue earned.

15 In theory it is possible to recognize revenue:
a As production takes place.
b When production is completed.
c When sale or delivery of the product is made or the services are rendered.
d As cash is collected from customers. In most cases, the accountant recognizes revenue at the time of sale of goods or the rendering of services.

16 Under special circumstances, accountants deviate from the realization principle. For example, the *percentage-of-completion* method of accounting for long-term construction projects recognizes revenue during production.

17 The timing of expense recognition is determined by the *matching principle.* Expenses may be recognized in two major ways: (a) in relation to the product sold or services rendered, (b) in relation to the time period during which revenue is earned.

18 *Consistency* is the principle which means that once an accounting method is selected, it will be constantly used and not changed from period to period. For example, if we used straight-line depreciation on our building last month, we should not switch to fixed-percentage-of-declining-balance this month. If we did, there would be a change in net income caused by the change in an accounting method rather than any real economic change.

19 The principle of *disclosure* means that all *material* (significant) and *relevant* facts concerning financial position and the results of operations must be communicated to the users of financial statements. This disclosure may be made either in the financial statements or in *footnotes* to the financial statements.

20 The concept of *conservatism* may not be an accounting principle, but it plays an important role in financial reporting. Conservatism means that when estimates must be made, the accountant will lean toward *understatement* of asset values and net income rather than toward overstatement.

21 The CPA conducts an audit of financial statements to render his opinion on whether the statements were prepared in accordance with *generally accepted accounting principles,* and present fairly the financial position and results of operations of the accounting entity. The CPA *does not guarantee* the accuracy of financial statements, but his *opinion* is highly regarded by users of those statements.

22 By combining transactions which take place during a period of rising (or fluctuating) price levels, accountants in effect ignore the "size" of the measuring unit—the dollar. Financial statements prepared in dollars having constant purchasing power are known as *common dollar* statements. The adjustment from historical to common dollars is made by using a *general price-level index.* This type of adjustment is *not* customarily made under current accounting practice.

23 Cash, receivables, and liabilities are reported at the same amounts in common dollar statements as in conventional statements. These are *monetary* items, and changes in price levels produce gains and losses as a result of holding these monetary items. If, for example, cash or accounts receivable is held while prices are rising, a purchasing power *loss* results; if money is owed during a period of rising price levels, a purchasing power *gain* results.

24 In a common dollar balance sheet, monetary items are shown at their face amount; nonmonetary items are *restated in the number of current dollars equivalent in purchasing power to the historical dollar amounts.*

25 In a common dollar income statement, revenue and expenses are restated in terms of current dollars. The income statement also contains a section showing the **gains or losses in purchasing power** resulting from holding monetary assets or owing money during changing price levels.

26 A conventional income statement measures the change in the **dollar amount** of stockholders' equity. A common dollar income statement measures the change in the **purchasing power** represented by stockholders' equity.

27 In periods of rising price levels, net income reported in common dollar terms may be smaller or larger than net income computed using conventional accounting procedures, depending on the relative amounts of monetary assets held and debts owed.

28 Statements prepared on a common dollar basis differ from those prepared using **replacement costs.** In preparing statements using replacement costs, the changing value of assets (as well as the changing value of the dollar) would be taken into account.

29 Financial statements adjusted for the changing value of money (or the changing value of specific assets owned) are currently prepared by only a few companies as **supplements** to financial statements prepared in conventional form. Accountants continue to search for the most effective means of reporting the impact of price-level changes on financial statements.

TEST YOURSELF ON ACCOUNTING PRINCIPLES

True or False

For each of the following statements, circle the T or the F to indicate whether the statement is true or false.

T F 1 Financial statements for companies in different industries should be prepared using the same accounting principles.

T F 2 **Generally accepted accounting principles** are well-established and not subject to change.

T F 3 The terms **postulates, principles,** and **standards** are essentially synonymous.

T F 4 An accounting entity is always a legal entity.

T F 5 Consolidated statements are prepared for an accounting entity which includes more than one legal entity.

T F 6 The going-concern principle means that a business is assumed to have an indefinite life and will continue to operate until all the firm's commitments have been satisfied.

T F 7 The preparation of periodic financial statements is necessary to provide decision makers with timely information.

T F 8 Dividing the life of a business enterprise into equal time segments makes the measurement process both more difficult and more tentative.

T F 9 The assumption that the dollar is a stable measuring unit is consistent with economic reality.

T F 10 Estimates of current market values may be more relevant but less reliable than historical costs for decision-making purposes.

T F 11 If a cash offer to buy land owned by a business is received and rejected, objectivity would require that the land be revalued to the amount of the offer.

T F 12 The principle of objectivity is made easier to apply because of the principle of periodic financial reporting.

T F 13 The cost principle and realization principle are both closely related to the need for objectivity.

T F 14 The realization principle states that revenue should not be recognized until the cash has been collected.

T F 15 The percentage-of-completion method recognizes revenue during the production process.

T F 16 **Consistency** means that all companies within a given industry (such as steel or petroleum) must use similar accounting procedures in the preparation of financial statements.

T F 17 Switching in midyear from lifo to fifo as a means of valuing inventory would be a violation of the principle of consistency and would require disclosure in the financial statements.

T F 18 The CPA prepares and guarantees the financial statements of his clients.

T F 19 Gains in the value of plant assets may be recognized as earned prior to sale if the market value of such assets can be objectively determined.

T F 20 If the general price level goes up, the value of money goes down.

T F 21 Owing money during an inflationary period would be advantageous to the borrower.

T F 22 All items on a common dollar balance sheet are restated in terms of an equivalent number of current dollars.

T F 23 Accountants have generally assumed that a firm is better off when it has recovered more than its original dollar investment in an asset.

T F 24 It is possible for a company to report a large net income using accepted accounting practices and a large loss when its financial statements are adjusted for the changing value of the dollar.

T F 25 The practice of converting accounting data into **common dollars** is not widely used in the United States.

T F 26 Replacement costs (fair market value) are not relevant for purposes of preparing **common dollar** financial statements.

Completion Statements

Fill in the necessary words or amounts to complete the following statements:

1 The most influential authoritative groups that have contributed to the development of generally accepted

accounting principles are: (a) _____

_____

_____, (b) _____

_____,

(c) _____

_____.

2 An underlying assumption that an accounting entity will continue in operation for an indefinite period of time sufficient to carry out its existing commit-

ments is called the _____ principle.

3 The term _____ refers to accounting measurements that are unbiased and can be veri-

fied; the term _____ assures users of financial statements that when a given accounting method is adopted, it will not be changed without adequate

_____ in the financial statements.

4 The cost principle calls for assets to be valued at

_____ rather than at _____ values.

5 The CPA conducts an _____ of the account-

ing system of a business and renders his _____

as to the _____ of the company's financial statements.

6 It would be theoretically possible to recognize the revenue of a business enterprise as realized at one

of the following points in time: (a) _____

_____, (b) _____

_____, (c)

_____

_____,

(d) _____

_____.

7 When the general price level increases, the

_____ _____ of the dollar

_____.

8 Financial statements prepared in terms of current dollars rather than historical dollars are referred to

as _____ _____ financial

statements.

Multiple Choice

Choose the best answer for each of the following questions and enter the identifying letter in the space provided.

_____ *1* Corporate managers are primarily interested in having financial data that:

a Are adjusted for changes in the value of assets and the value of money.

b Are objectively determined on a historical basis.

c Enable them to compare the results of their operations with those of other companies.

d Will aid them in making decisions.

_____ *2* Which of the following does not represent a generally accepted accounting principle?

a Accounting information is compiled for an accounting entity.

b Consistency in the application of particular accounting methods enables the user of accounting data to interpret changes in income or in financial position from period to period.

c The going-concern assumption justifies ignoring liquidating values in presenting assets in the balance sheet.

d Common dollar financial statements are the primary means of reporting to stockholders.

_____ *3* Financial statements prepared by a business firm are most likely to be:

a Fully reliable.

b Tentative in nature.

c Relevant for all types of decisions.

d Always misleading.

_____ *4* The independent accountant's opinion on a set of financial statements:

a Consists of three parts: a description of the scope of the audit, an opinion on the fairness of the statements, and a forecast of net income for the coming year.

b Can be issued only when the accountant has performed an audit of the statements and the accounting records.

c Can be issued if the accounting records have been maintained in a consistent manner even though the company has not followed generally accepted accounting principles.

d Guarantees to users that the statements have been prepared in accordance with generally accepted accounting principles and are free from any material error.

_____ 5 Revenue is most commonly recognized at the point that:

a Cash is collected.

b The order is received from customers.

c The sale is made.

d The production of manufactured goods is complete.

_____ 6 To qualify as "generally accepted," an accounting principle must receive substantial authoritative support. Many organizations and agencies have been influential in the development of generally accepted accounting principles, but the **most influential** leadership has come from the:

a Securities and Exchange Commission.

b AICPA.

c New York Stock Exchange.

d American Accounting Association.

_____ 7 Financial statements adjusted for changes in the purchasing power of the dollar:

a Restate all monetary items (such as cash and receivables) in terms of current-year dollars.

b Would cause land acquired in 1960 to be restated at an amount of fewer dollars than actual cost.

c Restate all nonmonetary items (such as land and buildings) in terms of current dollars.

d Will show a loss from borrowing during a period of rising prices.

_____ 8 During an inflationary period:

a Holding monetary assets will result in a purchasing power gain.

b The purchasing power which must be sacrificed to repay a liability of fixed amount is constantly decreasing.

c A purchasing power loss results from borrowing.

d The purchasing power of the dollar is constantly increasing.

_____ 9 Holding monetary assets of $1 million during an inflationary period results in a:

a Purchasing power gain.

b Purchasing power loss which is deductible for income tax purposes.

c Neither a purchasing power gain nor a purchasing power loss.

d Purchasing power loss, but no tax deduction.

Exercises

1 Within the current framework of generally accepted accounting principles, show the immediate effect upon total assets, liabilities, and owners' equity that would be recorded for each of the situations described below. Revenue and expenses are to be considered changes in owners' equity. Use the following code:

I = Increase, **D** = Decrease, **NE** = No effect

Situation	Assets	Liabilities	Owners' Equity
a An item with a long life and a material cost (a machine) is purchased for cash.			
b An item with a long life and an immaterial cost (a pencil sharpener) is purchased for cash.			
c An item of merchandise is acquired for cash at a price far below the price it will be sold for.			
d The item in c is sold for cash at a price above cost.			
e Cash is collected from a customer for a sale made last period.			
f Monetary assets are held during a period of inflation.			
g A contractor using the percentage-of-completion method of accounting for long-term contracts finds 10% of the costs have been incurred, and they total less than 10% of the contract price.			
h The contractor in g finds 40% of the costs have been incurred, and they exceed 40% of the contract price.			

2 Compute the **net** purchasing power gain or loss of the X Co. for a given period during which the general price level increased by 10% (from 100 to 110). In each case, the balance sheet for the X Co. remained unchanged during the period.

Case	Cash	Accounts Receivable	Inventory	Equipment	Liabilities	Capital Stock	Retained Earnings
a	$100,000					$80,000	$20,000
b	10,000	$40,000	$25,000	$25,000	$50,000	10,000	40,000
c			50,000	50,000	90,000	5,000	5,000

Case	Purchasing Power Gain	Purchasing Power Loss	Net Gain (or Loss)
a	$_____	$_____	$_____
b	$_____	$_____	$_____
c	$_____	$_____	$_____

3 In the space provided below, prepare a common dollar balance sheet for each case presented in Exercise 2.

X CO.
Common Dollar Balance Sheet
End of Month

Assets	a	b	c
Cash............................	$	$	$
Accounts receivable...............			
Inventory........................			
Equipment........................	_____	_____	_____
Total assets....................	$_____	$_____	$_____

Liabilities & Stockholders' Equity

	a	b	c
Liabilities........................	$	$	$
Capital stock.....................			
Retained earnings.................	_____	_____	_____
Total liabilities & stockholders' equity.	$_____	$_____	$_____

FIFTEEN

STATEMENT OF CHANGES IN FINANCIAL POSITION
CASH FLOWS

HIGHLIGHTS OF THE CHAPTER

1 We have seen how the income statement measures the profitability of a business. But profitability alone does not assure success; a business must also maintain adequate liquid resources to pay its maturing obligations and to take advantage of new investment opportunities. The **statement of changes in financial position** helps to measure the quantity and quality of resources employed by a business. This financial statement shows the **sources and uses of working capital,** and helps to answer such questions as: What use was made of net income? What became of the proceeds from a stock (or bond) issue? Is the company becoming more or less solvent?

2 The statement of changes in financial position has often been called a **funds statement** or a **statement of sources and uses of working capital.** The word **funds** is used to mean **all working capital,** not just cash.

3 A statement of changes in financial position measures changes in working capital. If working capital continued to decrease long enough, a business would become insolvent; excessive working capital means resources are not efficiently employed. In the short run, increases and decreases in working capital may be **independent of profitability.**

4 Sources of (increases in) working capital may come from (a) operations (revenue minus expenses that require funds), (b) sale of noncurrent assets, (c) borrowing by issuance of long-term notes and bonds, and (d) issuing additional shares of capital stock.

5 Working capital provided by operations consists of revenue minus expenses that require funds. This is the same thing as net income **plus expenses that did not require funds.** Examples of expenses that do not require funds are depreciation, amortization, and depletion. These items required funds when the **asset was acquired,** not when the expense was recognized through depreciation or amortization.

6 Extraordinary and nonoperating gains and losses (if material) should be **eliminated** from net income in computing the working capital provided by operations. This is because the working capital generated by the disposition of the asset causing the extraordinary or nonoperating gain or loss will **already be included** in the statement of changes in financial position as a source of working capital resulting from the disposition of a noncurrent asset.

7 Uses of working capital are (a) declaration of a cash dividend, (b) repayment of long-term debt, (c) purchase of noncurrent assets, and (d) repurchase of outstanding shares of capital stock.

8 Transactions involving only working capital accounts (current assets and current liabilities), such as short-term borrowing or the collection of an account receivable, **do not change** the amount of working capital (funds).

9 Transactions involving a working capital (current) account and a noncurrent account **must** either increase or decrease working capital. For example, the purchase of a building for cash **uses** working capital and long-term borrowing is a **source** of working capital.

10 Transactions involving only noncurrent accounts, such as the issuance of long-term debt in exchange

for a building, do not change the **amount** of working capital. This is because such an **exchange transaction** consists of both a **source** of working capital (the sale of bonds) and a **use** of working capital (purchase of a building). Since the source and the use of funds are equal, there is no change in the amount of working capital. Instead of ignoring these exchange transactions, a clearer picture will result if we include movements in financial resources in the statement of changes in financial position as **both** a source and a use of working capital.

11 Some transactions involving only noncurrent accounts, such as the distribution of a stock dividend or the retirement of a fully depreciated asset, are not exchange transactions and therefore their effect is not reported in the statement of changes in financial position.

12 It is not necessary to have a list of all transactions occurring during a period to prepare a statement of changes in financial condition. In practice, the statement is usually prepared on a working paper from analysis of changes in **noncurrent accounts** as presented in a **comparative balance sheet.**

13 The steps to be followed in preparing a statement of changes in financial position are (a) compute the change in working capital for the period, (b) prepare a working paper for analysis of changes in noncurrent accounts, and (c) prepare the statement of changes in financial position.

14 A working paper for analysis of changes in noncurrent accounts is prepared by listing the amount of working capital and the balances of the noncurrent accounts at the beginning of the period in the left-hand column, and the balances at the end of the period in the right-hand column. In the middle columns, the total change which has occurred in each account during the period is entered as a debit or a credit, and the resulting effect on working capital is listed below as a source or use of working capital. Each change in a noncurrent account generally results in a change in working capital.

15 After all the changes in noncurrent accounts have been recorded as changes in working capital, a total **increase** or **decrease** in working capital for the period is computed by **subtracting the uses of working capital from the sources of working capital.** This total increase or decrease in working capital should be the difference between the beginning and ending amounts of working capital listed in the working paper. (Carefully study the working paper for the Allison Corporation shown in your text.)

16 A statement of changes in financial position is prepared from the working paper once the net change in working capital has been confirmed. The statement consists of two parts: (1) the sources and uses of working capital, and (2) the composition of working capital at the beginning and the end of the period.

17 A statement of changes in financial position shows the inflow and outflow of liquid resources (working capital) during a period. However a company may have adequate working capital and still not be able to pay its debts if the working capital is primarily tied up in inventory and accounts receivable. Management may therefore prepare a **cash flow statement** which shows the reasons for the changes in the cash position of a business.

18 A cash flow statement shows (in summary form) all cash receipts and cash payments and the increase or decrease in cash during the period. Cash flow statements may be very useful in preparing **projected cash budgets.**

19 Much of a company's cash flow is generated by operations. A report of cash flow from operations can be prepared by converting the income statement from the accrual to the cash basis of accounting.

20 Revenue items can be adjusted to cash receipts by taking **net sales and subtracting any increase** (or adding any decrease) **in accounts receivable.** The cost of goods sold can be converted to cash payments for merchandise by **subtracting any decrease** (adding any increase) **in inventory** to find the total merchandise purchases and **subtracting any increase** (or adding any decrease) **in accounts payable.**

21 Expenses can be converted to the cash basis by two steps. From the listed expenses, (a) subtract any increase (or add any decrease) in accrued liabilities; and (b) add any increase (subtract any decrease) in short-term prepayments.

22 When depreciation expense is recorded, the offsetting credit is not to cash but to the Accumulated Depreciation account. The recognition of depreciation expense is not accompanied by a current cash payment.

23 When an income statement is restated to the cash basis, the net income figure will be converted to **cash flow from operations.** Sometimes cash flow from operations is referred to as **cash earnings** and is stated on a per-share basis. Cash earnings per share should not be confused with **earnings per share** (net income divided by number of shares outstanding). Cash flow, in the short run, may be independent of profitability.

TEST YOURSELF ON STATEMENT OF CHANGES IN FINANCIAL POSITION; CASH FLOWS

True or False

For each of the following statements, circle the T or the F to indicate whether the statement is true or false.

T F 1 The primary purpose of a statement of changes in financial position is to measure short-run profitability.

T F 2 The statement of changes in financial position is sometimes referred to as a funds statement.

T F 3 A statement of changes in financial position shows the sources and uses of working capital during an accounting period.

T F 4 In accounting terminology, the word *funds* is used to refer only to cash.

T F 5 Short-term borrowing may be a source of cash, but it is not a source of working capital.

T F 6 Selling a noncurrent asset is a source of working capital, even if the asset is sold at a loss.

T F 7 If the income statement shows a net loss for the period, there cannot have been any working capital provided by operations.

T F 8 A company which is profitable cannot have decreasing working capital.

T F 9 A company with decreasing working capital cannot be profitable.

T F 10 If a long-term liability is incurred for the purchase of a noncurrent asset, there will be no change in the amount of working capital, but the event will appear in the statement of changes in financial position as both a source and a use of working capital.

T F 11 A transaction that affects only current assets and current liabilities cannot cause a change in working capital.

T F 12 The payment of a cash dividend, not the declaration of the dividend, is a use of working capital.

T F 13 Transactions which affect a current asset or current liability account and a noncurrent account will cause a change in working capital.

T F 14 An increase in inventory is an application of funds (working capital).

T F 15 Depreciation expense is not a use of funds in the current period and should be added back to net income to determine working capital provided by operations.

T F 16 Extraordinary and nonoperating gains or losses are sources or uses of working capital and should be included in the amount of working capital provided by operations.

T F 17 A cash flow statement shows only receipts and payments of cash and does not show other changes in working capital.

T F 18 Net sales may be converted to cash received from customers by merely adding to net sales any decrease (or subtracting any increase) in receivables from customers.

T F 19 The delivered cost of net purchases may be converted to cash paid for merchandise by adding to net purchases any increase (or subtracting any decrease) in accounts payable to suppliers.

T F 20 An increase in accrued liabilities which is greater than the increase in short-term prepayments means that *more cash was paid* for expenses than is shown in the income statement.

Completion Statements

Fill in the necessary words or amounts to complete the following statements:

1 The statement of changes in _____ _____ shows _____ and _____ of _____ _____.

2 A statement prepared by management to analyze the sources and uses of cash is called a _____ _____ statement.

3 The _____ of a cash dividend is a _____ of working capital. The sale of a noncurrent asset at a loss is a _____ of working capital. Repurchase of outstanding capital stock, at a price below the original issue price, is a _____ of working capital.

4 Depreciation expense should be _____ to _____ _____ to determine working capital _____ _____ _____, because depreciation expense does not decrease working capital.

5 It is possible to prepare a statement of changes in financial position by analyzing the changes in _____ accounts.

6 A transaction which changes only _____ accounts cannot change the amount of working capital.

7 The cash flow from operations may be determined by converting an income statement from the _____ basis to the _____ basis of accounting.

8 To convert net sales to cash receipts from customers, you should add any _____ in receivables from customers. Expenses may be converted to the cash basis by adding any _____ in short-term prepayments and subtracting any _____ in accrued liabilities.

Multiple Choice

Choose the best answer to the following questions and enter the identifying letter in the space provided.

_____ **1** One of the following is not a use of working capital:

a Repayment of long-term debt.
b Acquisition of treasury stock.
c Cash dividend declared but not paid.
d Payment of an account payable.

_____ **2** Net income may be adjusted to show the working capital provided by operations by:

a Adding expenses not reducing working capital, adding extraordinary and nonoperating gains, and subtracting extraordinary and nonoperating losses.
b Adding expenses not reducing working capital, subtracting extraordinary and nonoperating gains, and adding extraordinary and nonoperating losses.
c Subtracting depreciation and amortization expenses.
d Adding any decreases in receivables and subtracting any increases in accounts and notes payable

_____ **3** Cash earnings per share of common stock:

a Has the same meaning as earnings per share.
b Should not be computed and published in audited financial statements.
c Is a reliable indicator of a company's profitability.
d Can be computed from information included in the statement of changes in financial position.

_____ **4** Purchases amount to $10,000, inventories increased by $4,000, and accounts payable decreased by $1,500. The cash paid to merchandise creditors was:

a $8,500
b $10,000
c $11,500
d $15,500

_____ **5** The purpose of a cash flow statement is to:

a Compute cash earnings per share.
b Explain increases or decreases in the cash balance from one date to another.
c Explain the reasons for changes in working capital.
d Restate net income on a cash basis.

_____ **6** Which of the following events appears in a statement of changes in financial position?

a Issuing long-term bonds payable in exchange for land.
b Purchasing inventory on credit.
c Repayment of a short-term loan.
d Distribution of a 10% stock dividend.

_____ **7** The composition of working capital at the beginning and end of a period:

a Appears in the working paper for statement of changes in financial position.
b Appears in comparative balance sheets and therefore should not be included in the statement of changes in financial position.
c Appears in the lower part of a statement of changes in financial position.
d Has little or no significance for users of financial statements.

_____ **8** When $1 million of bonds payable are converted into 40,000 shares of common stock, the statement of changes in financial position would include:

a Neither source nor use of working capital.
b Only a $1 million source of working capital, the issuance of common stock.
c Only a $1 million use of working capital, the retirement of bonds payable.
d A $1 million source and a $1 million use of working capital.

Exercises

1 The net income for the Lovelace Corporation in Year 1 amounted to $130,000 and included the following items:

Interest revenue.	$ 2,000
Depreciation expense.	40,000
Accrued salaries and wages expense.	4,000
Amortization of patents.	5,000
Gain on sale of plant assets (net of taxes).	20,000
Amortization of premium on bonds payable. . . .	2,500
Income tax expense.	80,500

In the space below, compute the working capital provided by operations:

Net income............................... $130,000
Add:

Subtotal............................. $ _____
Less:

$ _____

Working capital provided by operations...... $ _____

2 From the following information, prepare a statement of changes in financial position (without showing the composition of working capital) for Year 2 for the Fern Corporation:

a Net income for Year 2 was $175,000.

b Depreciation expense for Year 2 was $25,000.

c During Year 2, land which had cost $40,000 was sold for $60,000, net of the tax on the gain.

d A six-month bank loan of $50,000 made in Year 1 was repaid in Year 2.

e Additional equipment was acquired during Year 2 at a cost of $84,000.

f An earthquake caused $30,000 of damage to plant assets.

g A cash dividend of $42,500 was declared at the end of Year 2 to be paid in January of Year 3.

FERN CORPORATION
Statement of Changes in Financial Position
For Year Ended December 31, Year 2

Sources of working capital:
  Operations:
    Income before extraordinary items......... $ _____
    Add: _____
    Total working capital provided by operations. $ _____

$ _____
  Total sources of working capital.........

Uses of working capital:

$ _____
  Total uses of working capital........... _____
Increase in working capital............... $ _____

3 The financial statements for Z Company at the beginning and end of the current year are shown below:

Z COMPANY
Comparative Balance Sheets
Current Year

Assets	Ending	Beginning
Cash.........................	$ 55,000	$ 35,000
Marketable securities............	30,000	40,000
Accounts receivable.............	50,000	70,000
Inventory.....................	140,000	130,000
Plant and equipment (net of		
accumulated depreciation).....	415,000	330,000
Total assets..................	$690,000	$605,000

Liabilities & Stockholders' Equity

	Ending	Beginning
Accounts payable...............	$ 95,000	$ 30,000
Accrued liabilities..............	10,000	15,000
8% bonds payable...............	80,000	100,000
Capital stock..................	300,000	300,000
Retained earnings..............	205,000	160,000
Total liabilities & stockholders'		
equity....................	$690,000	$605,000

Z COMPANY
Income Statement
For Current Year

Net sales.....................................		$800,000
Cost of goods sold:		
Beginning inventory............	$130,000	
Purchases....................	500,000	
Goods available for sale........	$630,000	
Ending inventory..............	140,000	490,000
Gross profit on sales.................		$310,000
Expenses (includes depreciation of		
$15,000 and income taxes of		
$63,000)...............................		230,000
Net income............................		$ 80,000

Instructions

a Compute the working capital at the beginning of the current year..................... $ _____

b Compute the working capital at the end of the current year...................... $ _____

c Compute the increase (or decrease) in working capital during the current year...... $ _____

d In the space provided on following page, prepare a statement of changes in financial position for the current year. Assume that no items of plant and equipment were sold and that dividends of $35,000 were paid.

Z COMPANY
Statement of Changes in Financial Position
For Current Year

Uses of working capital:

Purchase of plant and equipment. . . . . $

Retirement of bonds payable. . . . .

Payment of dividends. . . . .   _____

   Total uses of working capital. . . . . $

Sources of working capital:

Operations:

Net income. . . . . $ _____

Add: Depreciations expense. . . . .

   Total working capital provided

     by operations. . . . .

Increase (decrease) in working   _____

  capital. . . . . $ _____

e Complete the following schedule:

Z COMPANY
Conversion of Income Statement from Accrual to Cash Basis
For Current Year

	Income Statement (Accrual Basis)	Add (Deduct)	Cash Basis
Net sales.	$800,000		
Add: Decrease in account receivable.			$
Cost of goods sold.	490,000		
Add: Increase in inventory.			
Less: Increase in accounts payable.	_____		_____
Gross profit on sales.	$310,000		$
Expenses.	230,000		
Add: Decrease in accrued liabilities.			
Less: Depreciation expense.	_____		_____
Net income.	$ 80,000		
Cash flow from operations.			$

f Complete the following cash flow statement:

Z COMPANY
Cash Flow Statement
For Current Year

Cash receipts:

Cash flow from operations—see part *e* above $

Sale of marketable securities. . . . .   _____

   Total cash receipts. . . . . $

Cash payments:

Purchase of plant and equipment. $

Retirement of bonds payable. . . . .

Payment of dividends. . . . .   _____

   Total cash payments. . . . .   _____

Increase in cash during the year . . . . $ 20,000

ANALYSIS OF FINANCIAL STATEMENTS

SIXTEEN

HIGHLIGHTS OF THE CHAPTER

1 *Financial statements* represent a report on managerial performance. In order to interpret the information contained in financial statements, the user should understand the working of the accounting system. Financial statements are of interest to many groups, each with a different set of needs.

2 Some sources of financial data available to users other than management include:

a Annual reports of corporations.

b Data filed with the Securities and Exchange Commission.

c Investment advisory services and stock brokerage firms.

d Organizations such as Moody's Investors Service, Standard & Poor's Corporation, and Dun & Bradstreet, Inc.

3 A given figure contained in financial statements is seldom significant to the reader; the *relationship* of figures, or the *change* since the end of the previous fiscal period, is generally much more useful.

4 The three most commonly used *analytical techniques* are:

a Dollar and percentage changes.

b Component percentages.

c Ratios.

5 *Dollar* and *percentage changes* are taken from *comparative* financial statements and give valuable clues to growth in working capital, sales, earnings, and other important trends affecting the business. The percentage relationship between any figure appearing in financial statements and the total which includes this figure (total assets in a balance sheet, and net sales in an income statement) is known as a *component percentage.* It can be used to measure the importance (or possible imbalance) of the item in question. A *ratio* measures the relationship of one financial item to another and calls attention to a significant relationship which may suggest further investigation.

6 In interpreting the significance of percentage changes, component percentages, and ratios, some *standard of comparison* should be used. Two widely used standards are:

a The past performance of the company.

b The performance of other companies in the same industry or the performance of the industry as a whole.

7 Comparison of data over time gives some idea of the company's performance compared with its past record and may be helpful in forecasting future performance.

8 Comparison of a company's performance with that of other companies similarly situated or with the aggregate results for an industry offers valuable clues to a company's ability to compete and perhaps to surpass the industry's performance.

9 The key objectives of financial analysis are to determine a company's *future earnings performance* and the *soundness and liquidity of its financial position.* To evaluate earnings performance and financial soundness, we are interested not only in the *amount* of earnings and assets, but also in the *quality of earnings,* the *quality of assets,* and the *amount of debt.*

10 The quality of earnings depends upon the *source* and *stability* of those earnings. The quality of earnings helps us to evaluate how likely it is that earnings will continue to grow or whether future earnings are likely to fluctuate widely. An analysis of the accounting principles and methods used by a company is helpful in evaluating the quality of earnings reported by the company.

11 A company may become insolvent even though it is profitable. The health and even the survival of a company may therefore be dependent not only on earnings, but also on the *quality of assets* and the *amount of liabilities* outstanding. A firm with inadequate cash position, slow-moving inventories, past-due receivables, and large amounts of short-term liabilities may be facing serious financial difficulties.

12 The analyst should evaluate the impact of inflation on the financial statements. He should try to measure the impact of the increase in general price level on net income, assets, and debt.

13 *Stockholders and potential investors* in the common stock of a company are primarily interested in the following:

a Earnings per share of common stock.

b Price-earnings ratio (the earnings rate).

c Dividends paid and the yield based on the market price of the stock.

d Book value per share of common stock.

e Revenue and expense analysis (the increase or decrease in specific revenue and expense items).

f The rate of return on the total assets used in the business.

g The rate of return on common stockholders' equity.

h Equity ratio (the proportion of total assets financed by stockholders).

14 Financing a business with fixed-return securities (bonds and notes payable and preferred stock) is known as *trading on the equity.* If the rate earned on total assets is *greater* than the rate paid on the fixed-return securities (the cost of borrowing), the common stockholders will gain from trading on the equity. Common stockholders will gain because the capital provided by the fixed-return securities is being invested to earn more than the amount which must be paid to the providers of that capital. The excess of the earnings generated by that capital over the fixed return paid out belongs to the common stockholders.

15 If the *return earned* on invested capital (return on assets) is *less* than the fixed return paid to the providers of that capital, the common stockholder will *lose* from trading on the equity.

16 The *debt ratio* (total liabilities ÷ total assets) measures the degree to which a company is trading on the equity. A high debt ratio means that a high percentage of the total assets is financed by creditors, and the company is trading heavily on the equity.

17 The *equity ratio* (stockholders' equity ÷ total assets) shows the percentage of total assets financed by stockholders. The equity ratio plus the debt ratio always equals 100%, so a low equity ratio means a high debt ratio. A low equity ratio may be profitable to common stockholders in periods of prosperity (when return on assets is greater than cost of borrowing), but it can lead to serious financial difficulties in a period of low earnings (if return on assets falls *below* the cost of borrowing).

18 *Long-term creditors* are primarily interested in the following measurements:

a The rate of return on investment, known as the *yield* on investment in bonds.

b The firm's ability to meet periodic interest requirements.

c The firm's ability to repay the principal of the debt at maturity.

19 The *yield* is computed by dividing the annual interest received on a bond (adjusted for amortization of bond premium or discount) by the market price of the bond. The safety of an investment in bonds depends on the ability of a firm to meet the interest and principal payments. The ability to pay interest is measured by the *times interest requirements were earned.* It is computed by dividing the income from operations by the annual interest expense. The safety of principal is, to some extent, measured by the *debt ratio.* The lower the debt ratio, the safer the position of creditors.

20 *Short-term creditors* are primarily concerned with the relationship of *liquid assets* to current liabilities and the *turnover* of accounts receivable and inventories. These are usually analyzed by computing the following:

a Working capital, the excess of current assets over current liabilities.

b Current ratio, current assets divided by current liabilities.

c Quick ratio, quick assets (cash, marketable securities, and receivables) divided by current liabilities.

d Liquidity ratio, highly liquid assets (cash and government securities) divided by current liabilities.

e Inventory turnover, cost of goods sold for the year divided by the average cost of inventory for the year.

f Turnover of accounts receivable, credit sales for the year divided by the average receivables for the year.

21 The *inventory turnover* and *accounts receivable turnover* may be expressed in *days,* by dividing 365 (days in a year) by the number of times the average inventory or receivables have turned over in one year.

TEST YOURSELF ON ANALYSIS OF FINANCIAL STATEMENTS

True or False

For each of the following statements, circle the T or the F to indicate whether the statement is true or false.

T F *1* The dollar amount of a change during a period in a certain item appearing in financial statements is probably less significant than the change measured as a percentage.

T F 2 Percentage changes are usually computed by using the latest figure as a base.

T F 3 It is possible that a decrease in gross profit rate may be more than offset by a decrease in expenses, thus resulting in an increase in net income.

T F 4 In a common size income statement, each item is expressed as a percentage of net sales.

T F 5 Industry standards tend to place the performance of a company in a more meaningful perspective.

T F 6 Two earnings per share figures frequently appear in an income statement: earnings per share before income taxes and earnings per share after income taxes.

T F 7 Earnings per share should be computed on the number of shares actually outstanding at the end of the period, regardless of changes in the number of shares during the period.

T F 8 If an extraordinary loss or a loss from discontinued operations appears in the income statement, the impact of these items on each share of common stock should be reported in the body of the income statement.

T F 9 Dividing the market price of a share of common stock by the dividend paid per share gives the price-earnings ratio.

T F 10 Book value per share generally indicates the amount each share of stock would expect to receive if the company were to be liquidated.

T F 11 The book value per share of preferred stock is widely used in evaluating the quality of both convertible and nonconvertible bonds.

T F 12 If some expenses are fixed (do not fluctuate in proportion to change in sales volume), net income should increase by a greater percentage than the increase in sales volume.

T F 13 If the rate of return on assets is substantially higher than the cost of borrowing, the common stockholder should want the company to have a high equity ratio.

T F 14 If a company gets into financial difficulty, both the debt ratio and the equity ratio might decline at the same time.

T F 15 The common stockholder will lose from trading on the equity when the cost of borrowing exceeds the return on assets.

T F 16 A high current ratio may indicate that capital is not productively used and that inventories and receivables may be excessive.

T F 17 It is possible to "doctor up" many balance sheet ratios by completing certain transactions just before the close of the fiscal period.

T F 18 Certain account balances at the end of the accounting period may not be representative for the entire year, and as a result the ratios (or turnover figures) may be misleading.

T F 19 In addition to ratios and other measurements, the growth potential of the company's products and the patent protection for major products should be taken into account in analyzing financial statements.

T F 20 The income statement measures all changes in the company's economic wealth during the period covered by the income statement.

Completion Statements

Fill in the necessary words or amounts to complete the following statements:

1 The three most widely used analytical techniques are _____ and _____ change, _____ _____, and _____.

2 The four groups that supply capital to a corporation are (a) _____ _____, (b) _____ _____, (c) _____ _____, and (d) _____ _____.

3 The reciprocal of the earnings rate of a company's stock is known as the _____ _____.

4 The debt ratio may be found by deducting the _____ _____ from 100%.

5 The current ratio is 3 to 1; working capital amounts to $100,000; and the quick ratio is 1.5 to 1. Compute the following: (a) current assets, $_____; (b) current liabilities, $_____; (c) total investment in inventories and short-term prepayments, $_____.

6 The number of times interest is earned is primarily important to _____ _____, and may be found by dividing _____ _____ _____ _____ by the annual _____ _____.

7 When the _____ _____ _____ is less than the cost of borrowing, common stockholders should prefer a _____ debt ratio.

8 Cost of goods sold during a year divided by the average cost of _____ gives the _____ _____ for the year.

Multiple Choice

Choose the best answer for each of the following questions and enter the identifying letter in the space provided.

_____ **1** An income statement showing only component percentages is known as a:

a Common dollar statement.

b Condensed income statement.

c Common size income statement.

d Comparative income statement.

_____ **2** One of the following **is not** a valuable standard of comparison in analyzing financial statements of a company engaged in the manufacture of mobile homes.

a Past performance of the company.

b Performance of another company engaged in the manufacture of mobile homes.

c Performance of all companies engaged in manufacture of mobile homes.

d Performance of companies engaged in construction of apartment buildings.

_____ **3** Common stockholders would be **least concerned** with one of the following:

a Earnings per share of common stock.

b Revenue and expense analysis.

c Book value per share.

d Quick ratio.

_____ **4** A company has a current ratio of 2 to 1 at the end of Year 1. Which one of the following transactions will **increase** this ratio?

a Sale of bonds payable at a discount.

b Declaration of a 50% stock dividend.

c Collection of a large account receivable.

d Borrowed cash from bank, issuing a 6-month note.

_____ **5** Bondholders would be **most** interested in one of the following:

a Quick ratio.

b Inventory turnover.

c Times interest earned.

d Cash flow from operations.

_____ **6** If sales increase by 10% from Year 1 to Year 2 and cost of goods sold increases only 6%, the gross profit on sales will increase by:

a 4%

b 10%

c 6%

d Some other percentage.

_____ **7** A useful measurement of a company's solvency is:

a Book value per share of common stock.

b Current ratio.

c Inventory turnover rate.

d Debt to equity ratio.

_____ **8** Baker Company has a large amount of quick assets and a relatively small amount of debt. During a period of rapid inflation, the company will:

a Gain from the increase in the general price level.

b Sustain a loss as a result of the inflation.

c Report a low rate of return on total assets.

d Have a low book value per share of common stock.

_____ **9** In projecting the future profitability of a merchandising company, investors generally will be least concerned with potential increases in:

a The rate earned on sales.

b The rate earned on total assets.

c Quick ratio.

d Sales volume.

_____ **10** Both a stock dividend and a stock split will:

a Reduce total stockholders' equity.

b Increase working capital.

c Increase book value per share of common stock.

d Reduce earnings per share of common stock.

Exercises

1 From the following comparative balance sheet for the Goldstream Company, compute the dollar and percentage changes from Year 1 to Year 2:

GOLDSTREAM COMPANY
Comparative Balance Sheet
Year 1 and Year 2

Assets	Year 2	Year 1	Increase (or Decrease) Amount	Percentage
Current assets...............	$150,000	$120,000	$	
Investments..................	160,000	80,000		
Plant and equipment (net).......	360,000	300,000		
Intangibles..................	80,000	100,000		
Total assets...............	$750,000	$600,000	$	

Liabilities & Stockholders' Equity

Current liabilities..............	$ 76,000	$ 80,000	$	
Long-term debt................	116,000	100,000		
Capital stock, $5 par...........	250,000	200,000		
Retained earnings..............	308,000	220,000		
Total liabilities & stockholders' equity.....................	$750,000	$600,000	$	

2 The balance sheets of the Oxnard Corporation at the beginning and end of Year 1 and the income statement for Year 1 are presented below:

OXNARD CORPORATION
Comparative Balance Sheet

Assets	Dec. 31, Year 1	Jan. 1, Year 1
Cash.........................	$ 60,000	$ 45,000
Marketable securities............	30,000	40,000
Accounts receivable (net).........	50,000	70,000
Inventory.....................	140,000	130,000
Plant and equipment (net of accumulated depreciation).............	420,000	330,000
Total assets................	$700,000	$615,000

Liabilities & Stockholders' Equity

Accounts payable................	$ 95,000	$ 30,000
Accrued liabilities...............	10,000	15,000
7% bonds payable..............	80,000	100,000
Capital stock, $5 par.............	300,000	300,000
Retained earnings*..............	215,000	170,000
Total liabilities & stockholders' equity.....................	$700,000	$615,000

*Dividends paid amounted to $0.65 per share.

OXNARD CORPORATION
Income Statement
For Year Ended December 31, Year 1

Net sales (all on credit).....................		$800,000
Cost of goods sold:		
Inventory, Jan. 1, Year 1........	$130,000	
Purchases....................	500,000	
Goods available for sale........	$630,000	
Inventory, Dec. 31, Year 1.......	140,000	490,000
Gross profit on sales...................		$310,000
Operating expenses (includes depreciation of $25,000).................		160,000
Income from operations..................		$150,000
Other expense: Bond interest expense........		7,000
Income before income taxes................		$143,000
Income taxes...........................		59,000
Net income............................		$ 84,000
Earnings per share......................		$ 1.40

On the basis of the information in the Oxnard Corporation financial statements, fill in the blanks below with the appropriate amounts (do not compute the ratios):

a The **current ratio** at the end of Year 1 would be computed by dividing $_____ by $_____.

b The **quick ratio** at the end of Year 1 would be computed by dividing $_____ by $_____ .

c The **accounts receivable turnover** during the year would be computed by dividing $_____ by $_____ .

d The **average inventory turnover** during the year would be computed by dividing $_____ by $_____ .

e The **number of times bond interest charges were earned** during Year 1 (before income taxes) would be determined by dividing $_____ by $_____ .

f The **rate earned on average investment in assets** would be determined by dividing $_____ by $_____ .

g The **equity ratio** at the end of Year 1 would be determined by dividing $_____ by $_____ .

h The **rate of return on the average stockholders' equity** would be determined by dividing $_____ by $_____ .

i The **earnings per share** of capital stock would be determined by dividing $_____ by _____ shares outstanding.

j If the capital stock had a market value at the end of the year of $42 per share, the **price-earnings ratio** would be determined by dividing $_____ by $_____ .

k The **yield** on the stock, assuming a market price of $42, is computed by dividing $_____ by $_____ .

l The **book value** per share of capital stock at the end of Year 1 would be computed by dividing $_____ by _____ shares outstanding.

m The **gross profit percentage** would be computed by dividing $_____ by $_____ .

n The **operating expense ratio** would be computed by dividing $_____ by $_____ .

3 Ten transactions or events are listed on page 102. Opposite each item is listed a particular ratio used in financial analysis. Indicate the effect of each transaction or event on the ratio listed opposite it. Use the following symbols: Increase = +; Decrease = −; No Effect = **NE**. (Assume that the current ratio and the quick ratio are higher than 1 to 1.)

Transaction or Event	Ratio	Effect
a Purchased inventory on open account.	Quick ratio	
b A larger physical volume of goods was sold at reduced prices.	Gross profit percentage	
c Declared a cash dividend of $1 per share.	Current ratio	
d An uncollectible account receivable was written off against the allowance account.	Current ratio	
e Issued additional shares of common stock and used proceeds to retire long-term debt.	Rate earned on total assets (before interest and income taxes)	
f Distributed a 20% stock dividend on common stock.	Earnings per share of common stock	
g Operating income increased 25%; interest expense increased 10%.	Times interest charges earned	
h During period of rising prices, company changed from fifo to lifo method of inventory pricing.	Inventory turnover	
i Paid previously declared cash dividend.	Debt ratio	
j Issued shares of common stock in exchange for plant assets.	Equity ratio	

SEVENTEEN

INCOME TAXES AND BUSINESS DECISIONS

HIGHLIGHTS OF THE CHAPTER

1 As the role of government in our society increases, so does the level of taxes. Taxes, which were almost insignificant in the early part of this century, now represent a major expense of doing business.

2 Because taxes have become such a significant expenditure, careful **tax planning** is essential to operating a business efficiently. Tax planning refers to determining in advance the income tax effect of every proposed business action, so the burden of taxes may be considered and minimized in the business decision.

3 In terms of revenue produced (to government), the four most important taxes are **income taxes, sales taxes, property taxes,** and **excise taxes.** Income taxes probably exceed all others and are most important in business decisions.

4 There are four classes of taxpayers: **individuals, corporations, estates,** and **trusts.** A **partnership** does not pay any income tax, but it must file an **information** return. Each partner includes his share of the partnership net income in his **personal** income tax return, regardless of the amount he withdraws from the business.

5 Almost all individual tax returns are prepared on the **cash basis** of measuring income. An individual may use the accrual basis if he chooses, but the cash basis is simpler, requires less record keeping, and permits tax savings by allowing the taxpayer to shift the timing of revenue and expenses from one year to another.

6 Taxes may be **proportional** (constant percentage of the base), **regressive** (decreasing percentage of the base as the base increases), or **progressive** (increasing percentage of the base as the base increases). Tax rates on individuals are highly progressive, ranging in recent years from 14% to 70% of taxable income.

7 Tax rates on corporations (in effect at the time this was written) were **normal tax,** 22% of all taxable income and **surtax,** 26% of all taxable income over $25,000.

8 Because of the progressive nature of individual taxes, an individual whose income fluctuates would have to pay more taxes than an individual who earned the same total amount at a more even annual rate. Therefore, individuals whose income fluctuates widely are permitted to average out their taxable income and to pay income taxes as if the income had been earned at an even rate over the last five years.

9 In analyzing the tax effect of a transaction, the **marginal** tax rate, not the **average** tax rate, should be used.

10 The income tax formula for individuals is as follows: Total income minus exclusions equals gross income. Gross income minus deductions to arrive at adjusted gross income equals adjusted gross income. Adjusted gross income minus deductions from adjusted gross income minus personal exemptions equals taxable income. The tax on the taxable income minus any tax credits equals the tax payable to the government.

11 Gross income of individuals includes **all items of income not specifically excluded by law.** Among the items **excluded** are:

a Interest on state and municipal bonds.

b Gifts and inheritances received.

c Life insurance proceeds resulting from death of insured.

d Workmen's compensation and sick pay.

e Social security benefits, pensions to veterans, and GI benefits.

f Compensation for personal damages.

g First $100 of dividends from domestic corporations ($200 on a joint return).

12 **Gains and losses from the sale or exchange of capital assets** are granted special treatment for income tax purposes. A gain or loss on the sale or exchange of capital assets held more than six months is a *long-term* gain or loss; the sale or exchange of capital assets held for less than six months results in a *short-term* gain or loss.

13 The amount of capital gain or loss included in the tax return for individuals is determined as follows:

a Long-term gains and losses are combined to produce a *net long-term gain or loss.* Short-term gains and losses are similarly combined into a *net short-term gain or loss.*

b If there is a net long-term gain and a net short-term gain, only 50% of the net long-term gain is included in taxable income, but 100% of the net short-term gain is included. Similar procedures are followed when the net gain (of either type) exceeds the net loss (of either type). A maximum tax rate, generally 25 to 35%, is levied on net long-term gains.

c If there is a net short-term loss and a net long-term loss, the short-term loss is combined with 50% of the long-term loss, and up to $1,000 of this total may be deducted to arrive at adjusted gross income. If the total exceeds $1,000, the excess may be carried to future tax years.

14 Deductions *to arrive at* adjusted gross income are:

a Business expenses.

b Employees' expenses.

c Expenses attributable to rents and royalties.

d Losses from the sale of property used in a trade or business and net capital losses up to $1,000 in any one year.

e Net operating loss carryovers from preceding years and 50% of net long-term capital gain.

15 Deductions *from* adjusted gross income are:

a The taxpayer may *itemize* and deduct certain expenditures in determining taxable income. These expenditures include interest, taxes, contributions, medical expenses (in excess of 3% of adjusted gross income), casualty losses (in excess of $100), and certain expenses relating to the production of income.

b As an *alternative* to itemizing deductions, the taxpayer is permitted to deduct a specific percentage of his adjusted gross income. This form of deduction is known as the *standard deduction.* The standard deduction at present is 15% of adjusted gross income. The standard deduction at present is limited to $2,000.

c *Personal exemptions* ($750 at present) may be deducted for the taxpayer, his spouse, and each dependent. A taxpayer and his spouse may each claim an additional exemption if he or she is blind, and another exemption if he or she is 65 years of age.

16 Individuals who compute their income on the calendar-year basis must file an income tax return by April 15 of each year. Corporations must file a return 2½ months after the end of their fiscal year.

17 The most common *credits* deducted from the taxes as computed on taxable income include:

a Amounts withheld or paid on declaration of estimated income tax.

b Retirement income credit.

c Taxes paid to foreign countries.

18 *Corporations* are not entitled to a personal exemption, standard deduction, or itemized deductions. Most itemized deductions by individual taxpayers are deductible by corporations as business expenses, except charitable contributions, which are limited to 5% of taxable income before contributions. Corporations cannot deduct a net capital loss; a net capital loss incurred by a corporation is first carried back three years and then forward five years and is offset against any capital gains.

19 Corporations are not entitled to the dividend exclusion of $100 allowed to individuals; corporations are, however, allowed to exclude 85% of the dividends they receive from other domestic corporations. Corporations are subject to a maximum tax rate of 30% on net long-term capital gains.

20 *Accounting income* often differs from *taxable income* because these amounts are computed with different purposes in mind. Furthermore, taxable income is computed by reference to specific laws, and laws generally do not govern the computation of accounting income.

21 A taxpayer usually can elect to use either the *cash* or the *accrual* basis of determining taxable income. When merchandise is a significant factor in a business, the accrual method is required. If the cash basis is used, depreciation must be computed in the same way as under the accrual basis, and income *constructively* received must be included in income even though cash has not been physically received.

22 The three major sources of differences between *accounting income* and *taxable income* are:

a *Special tax treatment* of revenue and expenses. (For example, municipal bond interest and 85% of intercompany dividends are excluded from taxable income. Political contributions and amortization of goodwill are not deductible expenses.)

b *Differences in timing* of revenue and expenses. (For example, income received in advance is taxed in the year of receipt; also certain expenses are not deductible for tax purposes until they are actually paid.)

c *Alternative accounting methods* for tax purposes and financial reporting (for such items as inventories, depreciation, installment sales, and research and development costs). Taxpayers will generally select an accounting method for income tax purposes that will minimize their current tax liabilities.

23 Significant differences between accounting income and taxable income may be caused by differences in timing of revenue and expenses or by using alternative accounting methods. *Income tax allocation* should be used to avoid the distortion of net income computed for financial reporting purposes. The objective of income tax allocation is to accrue income taxes in relation to accounting income, whenever differences between accounting and taxable income are caused by *differences in timing* of revenue and expenses (including those differences resulting from the use of alternative accounting methods).

24 Income tax considerations may be of great importance in making certain business decisions. Some of these decisions are:

a Choice of the form of business organization.

b Choice of accounting methods for inventories, plant and equipment, research and development costs, etc.

c Timing and manner in which property is sold.

d Allocation of values to assets when a business is acquired or sold.

e Types of securities to be issued in raising funds to finance a business.

TEST YOURSELF ON INCOME TAXES AND BUSINESS DECISIONS

True or False

For each of the following statements, circle the T or the F to indicate whether the statement is true or false.

T F **1** The cash basis of determining taxable income is more commonly used by individuals than the accrual basis.

T F **2** Individuals, corporations, and partnerships must all pay taxes on business income.

T F **3** An individual with a taxable income of $100,000 will pay more than twice as much tax as an individual with a taxable income of $50,000.

T F **4** Interest on municipal bonds, life insurance proceeds, social security benefits, and the first $100 of dividends from domestic corporations are examples of items which may be excluded from gross income for tax purposes by an unmarried taxpayer.

T F **5** The highest tax rate applied to a corporation is higher than the highest tax rate applied to individuals.

T F **6** Income averaging is designed to benefit individuals whose income is much higher in the current year than in the four previous years.

T F **7** A taxpayer with a net long-term capital gain of $3,000 and a net short-term capital loss of $5,000 may deduct $2,000 on his income tax return as a net short-term capital loss.

T F **8** A taxpayer with a net long-term capital loss of $1,800, and no net short-term gain or loss, has a $900 deduction to arrive at adjusted gross income.

T F **9** An individual may subtract items deductible to arrive at adjusted gross income and also take the standard deduction on the same income tax return.

T F **10** The taxpayer may itemize deductions from adjusted gross income and take the standard deduction on the same income tax return.

T F **11** An individual with an adjusted gross income of $20,000 may take a standard deduction of $3,000 under present rules.

T F **12** A full-time student earning $2,500 per year can qualify as a dependent for his parents.

T F **13** Corporations are not entitled to the standard deduction or a $100 dividend exclusion, but may deduct 85% of dividends received from other domestic corporations.

T F **14** If a taxpayer used the accrual basis to prepare his income tax return, his income for tax purposes would have to be the same as his accounting income.

T F **15** Planning a business transaction in advance to minimize the amount of income tax that will become due is termed tax avoidance and is usually illegal.

T F **16** Income received in advance is taxed in the year of receipt even though for accounting purposes it might be spread over several years.

T F **17** A taxpayer may not adopt for income tax purposes accounting methods which differ from those used for financial reporting.

T F **18** If the lifo method of inventory valuation is adopted for income tax purposes, it *must* be used in preparing published financial statements.

T F **19** Income tax allocation procedures tend to distort reported income because income taxes not yet due are reported as an expense in the income statement.

T F 20 Since corporations pay a lower rate of tax than a wealthy individual with a large taxable income, it may be advantageous for such individuals to incorporate their businesses and pay out only a small portion of earnings in the form of cash dividends.

Completion Statements

Fill in the necessary words or amounts to complete the following statements:

1 The four classes of taxpayers are _____, _____, _____, and _____.

2 In the United States, the four taxes which raise the most revenue for government are _____ tax, _____ tax, _____ tax, and _____ tax.

3 A partnership does not pay any tax but must file an _____ return.

4 Once an individual determines his adjusted gross income, he may either _____ _____ _____ or take the _____ _____ _____, and then take a _____ _____ for himself and each dependent.

5 If a taxpayer itemizes deductions, he may deduct _____, _____, _____, _____ _____ (in excess of 3% of adjusted gross income), _____ _____ (in excess of $100), and expenses relating to the _____ of _____.

6 Interest credited by a bank to a savings account represents taxable income to the recipient because it is _____ received.

7 A procedure designed to attain a better matching of pre-tax income and income tax expense for accounting purposes is known as _____ _____ _____.

Multiple Choice

Choose the best answer for each of the following questions and enter the identifying letter in the space provided.

_____ *1* The expression *tax planning* is usually taken to mean:

a The analysis of the tax consequences of alternative business decisions and the means of minimizing the income tax burden on the taxable entity.
b Preparing the various tax returns and making sure that cash is available to make the payments.
c The classification of various types of taxes in the accounts and the presentation in financial statements.
d Lobbying for the elimination of the double taxation of corporate income and dividends to stockholders.

_____ *2* Nolan has short-term capital gains of $2,000 and short-term capital losses of $3,000. He also has long-term gains of $6,000 and long-term losses of $1,000. The net amount of capital gains that he would include in taxable income is:

a $4,500
b $1,500
c $2,000
d Some other amount.

_____ *3* In determining whether the corporate or noncorporate form of business organization is preferable from an income tax standpoint for a small enterprise, which of the following factors would *favor incorporation:*

a The owner is the active manager of the business.
b The owner is single and withdraws most of the earnings of the business to meet his personal living expenses.
c The owner has substantial income from holdings of municipal bonds.
d The owner has substantial income from dividends on blue-chip stocks and prefers that earnings of the business be used to finance its expansion.

_____ *4* The cash basis of accounting:

a Cannot be used in filing income tax returns.
b Is widely used by manufacturing corporations.
c Should be used whenever possible since it postpones the payment of income taxes.
d Is permissible but usually results in a larger amount of income tax than does the accrual method.

_____ *5* The taxable income for an individual is determined as follows:

a Gross income less personal exemptions.
b Adjusted gross income less exclusions.
c Total income less exclusions less adjusted gross income.
d Adjusted gross income less standard deduction (or itemized deductions) less personal exemptions.

_____ *6* Hugh Dawson had an adjusted gross income of $16,000 on his joint tax return in Year 5 and $1,800 in personal expenses that qualify as deductions from adjusted gross income. Dawson has a wife who is not employed, and two small children. (The personal exemption is $750.) The taxable income Dawson should report is:

a $11,400
b $11,200
c $11,000
d $10,600

_____ **7** Sam has ordinary income of $12,200, a long-term capital gain of $4,000, and a short-term capital loss of $5,600. Based on these facts, Sam should report adjusted gross income for federal income tax purposes of:

a $10,600
b $13,200
c $8,600
d $11,200

_____ **8** Mann is considering a project that will result in increasing his taxable income from $20,000 to $24,000. His prospective tax without this additional income is $4,380, and with the extra income it would be $5,660. Based on these facts, Mann is subject to a *marginal* tax rate of:

a 23.6%
b 21.9%
c 28.3%
d 32%

_____ **9** Which of the following would *not* be a source of difference between *accounting income and taxable income?*

a Depreciation computed using different methods.
b Straight-line amortization of a patent over its useful life.
c Rental income received several years in advance.
d Inventory valuation using different methods.

Exercises

1 Both Robert and Betty Hill are 40 years old and have six dependent children, four of them by previous marriages. In preparing their income tax return for 19____, you obtain the following information:

Gross income:

Salary as vice president of food chain (before deductions)	$18,500
Dividends from domestic corporations (assume joint ownership)	580
Proceeds on life insurance policy upon death of Betty Hill's mother	5,000
Interest on City of Medford bonds	100
Interest on savings account	320
Gain on stock held over six months	8,000
Loss on stock held two months	(4,200)
Inheritance from father's estate	12,500
Christmas gift from family friend	50

Personal expenses:

Living expenses: food, clothes, etc.	7,800
Sales taxes, including tax on new car	400
State income taxes paid	300
Contributions to church and other allowable charities	300
Property taxes on residence and vacant lot	650
Federal excise taxes paid	150
Interest on mortgage and personal loan	1,320
Medical expenses	950
Subscription to investment advisory service	100
Gasoline taxes	60
Federal income tax withheld by employer	1,980
Social security taxes paid by employer	390

Instructions. Assuming that the standard deduction rate is 15% (with a limit of $2,000) and each personal exemption is $750, compute the taxable income that Robert and Betty Hill should report on a joint return.

ROBERT AND BETTY HILL
Computation of Taxable Income for 19_____

Gross income:

$

_____ $

Deduction to arrive at adjusted gross income:

_____

Adjusted gross income. . . . . $

Deductions from adjusted gross income:

Itemized deductions:

$

_____ $

Personal exemptions (_____ × $750). . . . . _____ _____

Taxable income. . . . . $ _____

2 The Harper Company reports income before income taxes of $200,000, which includes, among other items, the following:

Dividends from other corporations.	$20,000
Long-term capital loss.	8,000
Contributions to various charities.	2,000
Amortization of organization costs.	1,000
Amortization of goodwill.	5,000
Interest received on municipal bonds.	4,500

Compute below the income that would be taxable to the Harper Company at the normal and surtax rates:

Income before income taxes.	$200,000
Add:	
	$_____
Subtotal.	$_____
Less:	$_____
Taxable income.	$_____

3 The Riviera Construction Company is engaged in the construction of a dam over a three-year period. The company reports income for accounting purposes as construction progresses but waits until the job is completed to report the income for tax purposes. Relevant data follow:

	Year 3	Year 2	Year 1
Income before taxes for accounting purposes .	$ 20,000	$70,000	$10,000
Taxable income.	100,000	-0-	-0-
Income taxes paid, 40%.	40,000	-0-	-0-

Compute below the net income (after taxes) for each of the three years, assuming that *income tax allocation* procedures are followed:

Year	(a) Taxable Income	(b) Income Taxes, 40%	(a) − (b) Net Income
1	$_____	$_____	$_____
2	$_____	$_____	$_____
3	$_____	$_____	$_____

ANSWERS TO
QUESTIONS AND
SOLUTIONS TO
EXERCISES

CHAPTER 1

True or False

1 T *2* T *3* F *4* F *5* T *6* T *7* T *8* F *9* T
10 T *11* F *12* F *13* F *14* T *15* T

4 a Name of the company, *b* name of the statement, *c* date. *5* Audit. *6* Securities and Exchange Commission. *7* Internal control. *8 a* Profit, *b* solvent. *9* Creditors, stockholders, residual. *10* Assets, $80,000. *11* Understated, understated, correct. *12 a* Investment, *b* profits. *13* Increase. *14* Dividends, stockholders.

Completion Statements

1 Income statement, balance sheet. *2 a* Recording, *b* classifying, *c* summarizing. *3* Assets, liabilities, owners' equity.

Multiple Choice

1 b *2* c *3* a *4* c *5* c *6* a *7* b *8* d

Solutions to Exercises

1

TITAN CORPORATION
Balance Sheet
December 31, 19____

Assets		Liabilities & Stockholders' Equity		
Cash..............	$ 14,000	Liabilities:		
Accounts receivable....	37,000	Accounts payable...............		$ 28,000
Land................	35,000	Income taxes payable............		12,000
Buildings............	60,000	Total liabilities.................		$ 40,000
Office equipment.......	16,000	Stockholders' equity:		
Automobiles.........	8,000	Capital stock..........	$100,000	
		Retained earnings......	30,000	130,000
	$170,000			$170,000

2

UNITREX CORPORATION
Balance Sheet
December 31, 19____

Assets		Liabilities & Stockholders' Equity		
Cash..............	$ 42,000	Liabilities:		
Accounts receivable....	144,000[a]	Notes payable.................		$ 10,000[d]
Land................	90,000	Accounts payable.............		62,000[c]
Building.............	260,000	Income taxes payable...........		40,000
Office equipment.......	56,000	Total liabilities.................		$112,000
		Stockholders' equity:		
		Capital stock..........	$400,000[e]	
		Retained earnings......	80,000[f]	480,000[g]
	$592,000[b]			$592,000

[a] Accounts receivable must be $144,000 to achieve a total asset figure of $592,000.

[b] Total assets must be $592,000 to agree with the total of liabilities and stockholders' equity.

[c] Cash, $42,000, plus accounts receivable, $144,000, equals $186,000. Accounts payable are stated to be one-third of the combined total of cash and accounts receivable; that is, $186,000 ÷ 3 = $62,000.

[d] Total liabilities are given as $112,000 and consist of three items. One item, income taxes payable, is given as $40,000, and we have determined a second item, accounts payable, to be $62,000 (see footnote c). Therefore, notes payable must be $10,000; that is, $112,000 − $40,000 − $62,000 = $10,000.

[e] Capital stock equals stockholders' equity of $480,000 minus retained earnings of $80,000.

[f] Earnings are stated to be $100,000 and dividends $20,000; so retained earnings must be $80,000.

[g] Total liabilities and stockholders' equity is given as $592,000, and total liabilities as $112,000; therefore, the difference must be stockholders' equity of $480,000.

CHAPTER 2

True or False

1 F 2 T 3 T 4 T 5 T 6 F 7 F 8 T 9 F
10 F 11 T 12 T 13 F 14 T 15 F 16 T 17 T
18 F 19 T 20 F

Title, b debit side, c credit side. 4 Debits, credits, debits.
5 Left, debit, right, credit. 6 Cash, Notes Payable, debit,
credit. 7 Debit. 8 a Date, b account, debited, c account,
credited, d explanation. 9 L/P (ledger page), posted, numbers, cross-reference. 10 Trial balance, debit balances,
credit balances. 11 Book of original entry. 12 e, b, a, d, c.

Completion Statements

1 Left, ledger account, right. 2 Transaction, account. 3 a

Multiple Choice

1 a 2 c 3 b 4 d 5 c 6 b 7 c 8 a

Solutions to Exercises

1

Transaction	Account(s) Debited	Account(s) Credited
Example: Purchased land, paying part cash and signing a note payable for the balance.	3A	1B, 6C
1 Purchased office equipment on credit.	5A	7C
2 Collected the amount owed by a customer.	1A	2B
3 Borrowed money from the bank, signing a 90-day note.	1A	6C
4 Sold a portion of the land at cost for cash.	1A	3B
5 Returned a portion of the office equipment purchased in **1** above. The supplier agreed to credit Morrow Corporation's account.	7D	5B
6 Paid the balance of the amount due on the office equipment.	7D	1B
7 Issued additional capital stock for cash.	1A	8C

2

Cash

(1)	70,000	(3)	40,000
(2)	12,000	(7)	3,000

Land

(3)	30,000		

Building

(3)	60,000		
(5)	5,000		

Notes Payable

		(2)	12,000
		(3)	50,000

Accounts Payable

(6)	600	(4)	6,000
(7)	3,000	(5)	5,000

Capital Stock

		(1)	70,000

Office Equipment

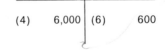

(4)	6,000	(6)	600

SUN CORPORATION
Trial Balance
September 30, 19____

	Debit	Credit
Cash	$ 39,000	
Land........................	30,000	
Building.....................	65,000	
Office equipment.............	5,400	
Notes payable...............		$ 62,000
Accounts payable.............		7,400
Capital stock................		70,000
	$139,400	$139,400

CHAPTER 3

True or False

1 T *2* T *3* F *4* T *5* F *6* T *7* F *8* T *9* T
10 T *11* T *12* F *13* T *14* T *15* F *16* F *17* F
18 F

Completion Statements

1 $49,000; $68,000; $57,000. *2* Dividends, Dividends Payable, Dividends Payable, Cash. *3* Profits, losses, investment. *4* Revenue, expense. *5* Cost, depreciation. *6* Closing entries. *7* Retained Earnings, credits. *8* Producing revenue, decrease, owners' equity.

Multiple Choice

1 c *2* a *3* b *4* c *5* d *6* c *7* a *8* b

Solutions to Exercises

1a

MISSION AUTO REPAIR, INC.
Income Statement
For the Month Ended May 31, 19___

Repair revenue.........................		$27,000
Expenses:		
Rent.......................	$ 2,000	
Wages........................	11,000	
Advertising..................	1,400	
Utilities......................	300	
Depreciation..................	700	
Total expenses....................		15,400
Net income............................		$11,600

1b

MISSION AUTO REPAIR, INC.
Statement of Retained Earnings
For the Month Ended May 31, 19___

Retained earnings, Apr. 30, 19___	$40,000
Net income................................	11,600
Total....................................	$51,600
Dividends................................	8,000
Retained earnings, May 31, 19___	$43,600

1c

MISSION AUTO REPAIR, INC.
Balance Sheet
May 31, 19___

Assets

Cash....................................		$21,600
Notes receivable.......................		4,000
Accounts receivable.....................		42,000
Garage equipment..............	$33,600	
Less: Accumulated depreciation....	9,100	24,500
Total assets.........................		$92,100

Liabilities & Stockholders' Equity

Liabilities:		
Notes payable........................		$ 8,200
Accounts payable.....................		10,300
Total liabilities....................		$18,500
Stockholders' equity:		
Capital stock.................	$30,000	
Retained earnings..............	43,600	73,600
Total liabilities & stockholders' equity.......		$92,100

CHAPTER 4

True or False

1 T *2* F *3* F *4* T *5* T *6* T *7* F *8* T *9* F
10 F *11* T *12* T *13* F *14* F *15* T *16* T *17* T
18 F *19* F *20* F

Completion Statements

1 Recorded costs, unrecorded expenses, recorded revenue, unrecorded revenue. *2 a* Allocates, expense, *b* asset, Unexpired Insurance. *3* Revenue, expense. *4* Debit, expense, credit, asset. *5* Debit, asset, credit, liability. *6* Debit, expense, credit, liability. *7* Debit, expense, credit, asset, liability. *8* Debit, asset, asset, liability. *9* Debit, credit, debits, credits, credit. *10* Commissions Receivable, Commissions Earned, Cash, Commissions Receivable, $200, Commissions Earned, $200.

Multiple Choice

1 b *2* a *3* c *4* c *5* c *6* a *7* d *8* d *9* b *10* c

2

Error	Total Revenue	Total Expense	Net Income	Total Assets	Total Liabilities	Total Owners' Equity
1	NE	U	O	O	NE	O
2	O	NE	O	O	NE	O
3	NE	U	O	O	NE	O
4	NE	NE	NE	NE	U	O
5	NE	U	O	O	NE	O
6	NE	NE	NE	NE	NE	NE

Solutions to Exercises

1

	Trial Balance Debit	Trial Balance Credit	Adjustments Debit	Adjustments Credit	Adjusted Trial Balance Debit	Adjusted Trial Balance Credit	Income Statement Debit	Income Statement Credit	Retained Earnings Debit	Retained Earnings Credit	Balance Sheet Debit	Balance Sheet Credit
Cash	4,800				4,800						4,800	
Accounts receivable	17,600				17,600						17,600	
Unexpired insurance	360			a 60	300						300	
Office supplies	1,900			b 650	1,250						1,250	
Office equipment	4,800				4,800						4,800	
Accumulated depreciation: office equipment		560		c 40		600						600
Notes payable		8,000				8,000						8,000
Accounts payable		1,800				1,800						1,800
Unearned commissions		1,500	e 800			700						700
Capital stock		9,000				9,000						9,000
Retained earnings, June 1, 19___		7,000				7,000				7,000		
Dividends	1,000				1,000				1,000			
Commissions earned		16,000		e 800		16,800		16,800				
Rent expense	2,400				2,400		2,400					
Salaries expense	11,000		f 200		11,200		11,200					
	43,860	43,860										
Insurance expense			a 60		60		60					
Office supplies expense			b 650		650		650					
Depreciation expense: office equipment			c 40		40		40					
Interest expense			d 50		50		50					
Interest payable				d 50		50						50
Salaries payable				f 200		200						200
			1,800	1,800	44,150	44,150	14,400	16,800				
Net income							2,400			2,400		
							16,800	16,800	1,000	9,400		
Retained earnings, June 30, 19___									8,400			8,400
									9,400	9,400	28,750	28,750

2

General Journal

19___	Adjusting Entries		
	a		
June 30	Insurance Expense	60	
	Unexpired Insurance		60
	To record insurance expired during June.		
	b		
30	Office Supplies Expense	650	
	Office Supplies		650
	To record consumption of office supplies during		
	June.		
	c		
30	Depreciation Expense: Office Equipment	40	
	Accumulated Depreciation: Office Equipment		40
	Depreciation expense for June ($4,800 ÷ 120 months).		
	d		
30	Interest Expense	50	
	Interest Payable		50
	To record interest expense for June.		
	e		
30	Unearned Commissions	800	
	Commissions Earned		800
	To record commissions earned during June.		
	f		
30	Salaries Expense	200	
	Salaries Payable		200
	To record salary expense and related liability at		
	June 30.		
	Closing Entries		
30	Commissions Earned	16,800	
	Income Summary		16,800
	To close the revenue account.		
30	Income Summary	14,400	
	Rent Expense		2,400
	Salaries Expense		11,200
	Insurance Expense		60
	Office Supplies Expense		650
	Depreciation Expense: Office Equipment		40
	Interest Expense		50
	To close the expense accounts.		
30	Income Summary	2,400	
	Retained Earnings		2,400
	To close the Income Summary account.		
30	Retained Earnings	1,000	
	Dividends		1,000
	To close the Dividends account.		

CHAPTER 5

True or False

1 F *2* T *3* F *4* T *5* T *6* F *7* T *8* T *9* F
10 F *11* T *12* T *13* T *14* T *15* T *16* F *17* T
18 F *19* F *20* F *21* T

Completion Statements

1 Internal control. *2* Cost of goods available for sale, ending inventory, cost of goods sold. *3* Sales Returns & Allowances, Cash, Accounts Receivable. *4* $1,960; $1,960; debit, Sales Discounts, $40; Accounts Receivable, $2,000. *5* Periodic inventory, Purchases, debited. *6* Credit, debit, Income Summary, Inventory, Income Summary. *7* A deduction from sales, a deduction from purchases. *8* Current assets, plant and equipment, other assets, current liabilities, long-term liabilities. *9* Operating cycle. *10* Working capital, current ratio, solvency.

Multiple Choice

1 d *2* b *3* b *4* a *5* c *6* d *7* a *8* d *9* d
10 d

Solutions to Exercises

1

	Ending Inventory	Cost of Goods Sold	Gross Profit on Sales	Net Income
a	U	O	U	U
b	NE	O	U	U
c	NE	O	U	U
d	NE	U	O	O
e	NE	U	O	O
f	O	U	O	O
g	NE	U	O	O
h	NE	NE	U	U

2

Sales		$161,000
Sales returns & allowances	$ 4,500	
Sales discounts	1,500	6,000
Net sales		$155,000
Cost of goods sold.		
Inventory, Jan. 1		$ 22,000
Purchases	$ 98,500	
Transportation-in	3,600	
Delivered cost of purchases	$102,100	
Purchase returns & allowances	$3,100	
Purchase discounts	2,000 5,100	
Net purchases	97,000	
Cost of goods available for sale	$119,000	
Inventory, Dec. 31	26,000	
Cost of goods sold		93,000
Gross profit on sales		$ 62,000
Operating expenses		46,500
Net income		$ 15,500

CHAPTER 6

True or False

1 F *2* F *3* F *4* T *5* T *6* T *7* F *8* T *9* F
10 T *11* T *12* F *13* F *14* F *15* F *16* F *17* T
18 F *19* F *20* F *21* T

Completion Statements

1 Posting. *2* Purchases, general, debit. *3* Debit, Accounts Receivable, credit, Sales. *4* Sales invoices, invoices, general, controlling. *5* Program. *6* Punched cards, paper tape, magnetic tape. *7* Output, input, hardware, software. *8* Not be posted. *9* Occurs frequently. *10* Control total, limit test. *11* Time sharing, terminal. *12* Integrated.

Multiple Choice

1 d *2* a *3* c *4* a *5* c *6* b *7* b *8* c

Solutions to Exercises

1 a	S
b	CP
c	CP
d	CR
e	J
f	J
g	J
h	CP
i	J
j	CR
k	P
l	J
m	J
n	J

2	Debit	Credit
a	P, CP	J
b	J	J, CR
c	J	CP
d	J	S, CR
e	J, CP	J
f	CR	J
g	J, CP	P, J
h	S	CR, J
i	CR	CP
j	J	J

CHAPTER 7

True or False

1 T *2* F *3* T *4* F *5* F *6* F *7* F *8* T *9* T
10 T *11* F *12* F *13* T *14* T *15* T *16* F *17* T
18 F *19* F *20* T

Completion Statements

1 Cost. *2* Corporation, single proprietorship, partnership.
3 $20,000; 3-1. *4* ($2,000) loss, $8,000. *5* $9,000. *6 a*
Heavy taxation, *b* greater regulation. *7 a* Incorporation
fee paid to the state, *b* legal fees, *c* payments to promoters.
8 a Bylaws, *b* minutes, *c* annual report. *9* Preferred Stock,
Common Stock, Paid-in Capital in Excess of Par. *10*
$400,000; $80,000; $118,000.

Multiple Choice

1 d *2* b *3* c *4* c *5* b *6* b *7* b *8* b *9* a *10* c

Solutions to Exercises

		A's Share	B's Share
1 First situation:	a	$ 4,000	$ 6,000
	b	6,550	3,450
	c	5,350	4,650
Second situation:	a	$(2,000)	$(2,000)
	b	600	(4,600)

2 Net income for Year 2 . . . . $180,000
 Less: Deficit at beginning of Year 2 20,000
 Retained earning available for dividends $160,000
 Less: Dividends on preferred stock for 2
  years (10,000 × $10) 100,000
 Available for common stock . . . . $ 60,000
 Less: Balance in retained earnings at end of
  Year 2 25,000
 Dividends paid on common stock . . . . $ 35,000
 Dividends per share: $35,000 ÷ 10,000 . . . . . $3.50

3 a Income Summary 15,000
  K, Capital 9,000
  L, Capital 6,000

  K, Capital 10,000
   K, Drawing 10,000

  L, Capital 4,000
   L, Drawing 4,000

b

K & L
Statement of Partners' Capitals
For Year 1

	K	L	Total
Balance, beginning of year . .	$18,400	$17,750	$36,150
Add: Net income for year . . .	9,000	6,000	15,000
Subtotal	$27,400	$23,750	$51,150
Less: Withdrawals	10,000	4,000	14,000
Balance, end of year	$17,400	$19,750	$37,150

4 a Organization Costs 6,000
  Cash 6,000

 b Equipment 30,000
  Capital Stock 20,000
  Paid-in Capital in Excess of
   Par 10,000

 c Dividends 25,000
  Dividends Payable 25,000

 d Dividends Payable 25,000
  Cash 25,000

5 Stockholders' equity:

$4 preferred stock, $100 par, 1,000 shares issued and outstanding.............	$100,000
Common stock, no-par value, 50,000 shares issued and outstanding.........	200,000
Paid-in capital in excess of par: preferred stock...........................	10,000
Total paid-in capital................	$310,000
Retained earnings....................	128,000
Total stockholders' equity...........	$438,000

CHAPTER 8

True or False

1 F **2** T **3** T **4** T **5** F **6** F **7** F **8** T **9** T
10 F **11** T **12** T **13** T **14** T **15** F **16** T **17** F
18 T **19** T **20** F

Completion Statements

1 Income, extraordinary items. **2** Primary, fully diluted.
3 Options, convertible bonds, convertible preferred stock.
4 Note. **5** a $1,020,000; b $440,000; c $740,000. **6** a
$900,000; b $0.20; c before; d $2,358,800; e $21
[($103,400 + $94,000) ÷ 9,400 shares].

7

Transaction or Event	In-crease	De-crease	No Effect
a Declaration of cash dividend		✔	
b Distribution of a 20% stock dividend..................		✔	
c A 4 for 1 stock split........		✔	
d Net income is reported for latest year...............	✔		
e Additional stock is sold at $15 per share.............	✔		
f Treasury stock is acquired at $6 per share............	✔		
g Additional shares are authorized....................			✔
h Par value of $5 per share is changed to stated value of $1 per share..............			✔

Multiple Choice

1 d **2** d **3** d **4** c **5** e **6** a **7** d **8** c **9** c
10 b

Solutions to Exercises

1
BOOKER COMPANY
Statement of Retained Earnings
For Year 10

Retained earnings at beginning of year:		
As originally reported.................		$1,221,000
Add: Prior period adjustment—amount received in settlement of lawsuit initiated in Year 6..........................		375,000
As restated..........................		$1,596,000
Add: Net income......................		294,000
Subtotal..........................		$1,890,000
Less: Cash dividends.........	$ 40,000	
Stock dividend.........	150,000	190,000
Retained earnings at end of year...........		$1,700,000

2 a $700,000 ($200,000 + $500,000)
  b $8.75 ($17,500 ÷ 2,000)
  c $10.50 [($200,000 + $10,000) ÷ 20,000]
  d $7.50 [($500,000 + $250,000) ÷ 100,000]
  e $10.00 [($1,200,000 − $220,000) ÷ 98,000]

3	General Journal		
Year 1			
Mar. 1	Dividends	200,000	
	Dividends Payable		200,000
	Declared cash dividend of $0.80 per share on 250,000 shares.		
21	Dividends Payable	200,000	
	Cash		200,000
Aug. 10	Retained Earnings	500,000	
	Stock Dividend to Be Distributed		62,500
	Paid-in Capital from Stock Dividends		437,500
	Declared 5% stock dividend on 250,000 shares of $5 par value		
	stock.		
Sept. 2	Stock Dividend to Be Distributed	62,500	
	Common Stock		62,500
Dec. 21	Retained Earnings	1,312,500	
	Common Stock		1,312,500
	Declared and issued 100% stock dividend on 262,500 shares of		
	$5 par stock.		
30	Treasury Stock	30,000	
	Cash		30,000

CHAPTER 9

True or False

1 T 2 F 3 T 4 T 5 F 6 T 7 T 8 T 9 F
10 F 11 T 12 T 13 F 14 T 15 F 16 F 17 F
18 T 19 T 20 T

Completion Statements

1 Checks, bank accounts. 2 Maintenance of accounting records. 3 Cash payments. 4 Deposited intact in the bank. 5 Collusion of two or more persons. 6 Outstanding checks, deposits in transit. 7 Not Sufficient Funds, Accounts Receivable. 8 Deducted from, bank statement, added to, bank statement, deducted from, depositor's records, added to, depositor's records. 9 92½. 10 Accrued Bond Interest Receivable. 11 Income, cost basis. 12 Debiting, crediting, Gain from Increase in Market Value of Securities, Unrealized Gain on Marketable Securities, Neither.

Multiple Choice

1 d 2 c 3 c 4 c 5 a 6 c 7 c 8 b 9 b
10 a 11 b 12 b

Solutions to Exercises

1

HUNTER CORPORATION
Bank Reconciliation
July 31, 19____

Balance per depositor's records, July 31, 19____			$11,364
Add: Note receivable collected for us by bank.			1,800
			$13,164
Deduct: Service charge	$ 6		
NSF check of Jay Kline	264		
Error on check no. 295	108		378
Adjusted balance			$12,786
Balance per bank statement, July 31, 19____ .			$17,018
Add: Deposit of July 31			1,950
			$18,968
Deduct: Outstanding checks:			
No. 301		$2,500	
No. 303		600	
No. 304		1,800	
No. 306		1,282	6,182
Adjusted balance (as above)			$12,786

2

19___	General Journal		
June 30	Cash	1,800	
	Notes Receivable		1,800
	To record collection of note receivable for us by bank and credit		
	to our account.		
30	Miscellaneous Expense	6	
	Cash		6
	To record service charge by bank.		
30	Accounts Receivable, Jay Kline	264	
	Cash		264
	To record as a receivable the NSF check returned by bank.		
30	Accounts Payable (or Accounts Receivable)	108	
	Cash		108
	To record claim against supplier of office supplies because of		
	accidental overpayment of an invoice.		

3

1976	General Journal		
Sept. 1	Accrued Bond Interest Receivable	500	
	Investment in Bonds	88,250	
	Cash		88,750
	Purchased $100,000 par value of World Airlines 6% bonds of 1998		
	at 87¾ and accrued interest, plus commission of $500.		
Dec. 31	Accrued Bond Interest Receivable	2,000	
	Bond Interest Earned		2,000
	To accrue bond interest earned to Dec. 31 ($100,000 $\times$ 6% $\times$ 4/12).		
1977			
Feb. 1	Cash	3,000	
	Accrued Bond Interest Receivable		2,500
	Bond Interest Earned		500
	Received semiannual bond interest on World Airlines bonds ($100,000		
	$\times$ 6% $\times$ ½).		
Apr. 1	Accrued Bond Interest Receivable	1,000	
	Bond Interest Earned		1,000
	To accrue interest to date of sale of investment in World Airlines		
	bonds ($100,000 $\times$ 6% $\times$ 2/12).		
Apr. 1	Cash	91,500	
	Investment in Bonds		88,250
	Accrued Bond Interest Receivable		1,000
	Gain on Sale of Investments		2,250
	To record sale of $100,000 par value of World Airlines 6% bonds of		
	1998 at 91 plus accrued interest of $1,000 and minus commission of		
	$500.		

CHAPTER 10

True or False

1 T *2* T *3* F *4* T *5* F *6* T *7* T *8* F *9* T
10 T *11* T *12* F *13* F *14* F *15* T *16* F *17* T
18 T *19* T *20* F *21* T

Completion Statements

1 Matching costs and revenue, net income. *2* Overstated, overstated, overstated. *3* Uncollectible accounts expense, allowance for uncollectible accounts. *4* $15,940; debit, Interest Expense, $60; $16,000. *5* 7½%. *6* Accrued Interest Receivable, Interest Earned, Interest Earned. *7* $4,032; debit, Credit Card Discount Expense, $168; credit, Accounts Receivable—Global Express, $4,200. *8* Contra-liability, deducted, interest expense. *9* Contra-asset, deducted, notes receivable, interest earned. *10* $10,075; $10,075; $10,150; $10,150.

Multiple Choice

1 d *2* a *3* d *4* d *5* a *6* b *7* c *8* c

Solutions to Exercises

1

Accounts	
Debited	Credited
A, C	X
1	D	C
2	A	E
3	A, J	C
4	A, I	B
5	C	D
6	I	G
7	A, F	E
8	A	C
9	E, G, I	A
10	I	F

2 a $124.50
b $126.00
c $ 90.00
d $120.00
e $130.00

CHAPTER 11

True or False

1 T *2* T *3* T *4* F *5* T *6* T *7* F *8* F *9* F
10 T *11* T *12* F *13* F *14* F *15* F *16* T *17* T
18 T *19* F *20* F *21* T *22* T

Completion Statements

1 Title, seller, buyer. *2* $5,000; $37,000; $18,000. *3 a* Specific identification, *b* average cost, *c* first-in, first-out; *d* last-in, first-out. *4* Fifo, largest. *5* Replacement cost, reinvested, inventory, fifo. *6* Decrease, replacement, increase, replacement. *7* Lifo, *8* Retail, cost, ratio, or percentage. *9 a* Raw materials, *b* goods in process, *c* finished goods. *10 a* $50,000. ($450,000 − $400,000); *b* $120,000 ($400,000 − $80,000 − $200,000); *c* $430,000 ($450,000 − $20,000); *d* $437,500 ($430,000 + $7,500).

Multiple Choice

1 b *2* c *3* b *4* a *5* d *6* b *7* b *8* c

Solutions to Exercises

		Inventory	Cost of Goods Sold
1	*a*	$ 6,300	$ 16,600
	b	$ 6,250	$ 16,650
	c	$ 5,000	$ 17,900
	d	$ 5,725	$ 17,175

2 Physical inventory, July 10, 19____ $30,000
Less: Net purchases for period July 1–10
($17,500 − $550)................... 16,950
$13,050
Add: Cost of goods sold for period July 1–10:
$15,200 − $400 = $14,800 net sales;
$14,800 × 77.5% (cost percentage)..... 11,470
Approximate inventory, June 30, 19____ $24,520

3

ALLISON COMPANY
Comparative Income Statement
For Years 1, 2, and 3

	Year 3	Year 2	Year 1
Sales.	$540,000	$506,000^a	$504,000^b
Cost of goods sold:			
Beginning inventory.	$ 40,000^c	$ 45,000	$ 30,000
Purchases.	407,500	380,000	375,000
Cost of goods available for sale.	$447,500	$425,000	$405,000
Less: Ending inventory	60,000	40,000^c	45,000
Cost of goods sold.	$387,500	$385,000	$360,000
Gross profit on sales.	$152,500	$121,000	$144,000
Expenses^d.	70,000	75,000	120,000
Net income.	$ 82,500	$ 46,000	$ 24,000

a Cost of goods sold (as reported), $375,000, plus gross profit on sales (as reported), $135,000, less sale of Year 1, $4,000 erroneously reported in Year 2.

b Cost of goods sold (as reported), $360,000, plus gross profit on sales (as reported), $140,000, plus sale of $4,000 erroneously reported in Year 2.

c $50,000 (as reported) less overstatement of $10,000.

d Gross profit on sales (as reported), less net income (as reported).

CHAPTER 12

True or False

1 T *2* T *3* F *4* T *5* F *6* F *7* T *8* F *9* F
10 F *11* T *12* F *13* T *14* T *15* T *16* F *17* T
18 F *19* F *20* T *21* T *22* T *23* F *24* T

Completion Statements

1 a Physical deterioration, *b* obsolescence. *2* Capital, revenue, understated. *3* $40,000; $35,000; $37,000. *4* Extend, useful life, Accumulated Depreciation. *5* Original cost, Accumulated Depreciation. *6* Book value, additional amount. *7* Physical substance, current asset, amortization. *8* Present value, excess, paid for.

Multiple Choice

1 c *2* a *3* b *4* c *5* d *6* c *7* d *8* c *9* c

Solutions to Exercises

1	Year 1	Year 2
a ($11,000 − $1,000) × ¼ × $\frac{9}{12}$...	$1,875	
$10,000 × ¼.		$2,500
b 20,000 × 10 cents.	$2,000	
40,000 × 10 cents.		$4,000
c $10,000 × $\frac{4}{10}$ × $\frac{9}{12}$.	$3,000	
$10,000 × $\frac{4}{10}$ × $\frac{3}{12}$ + ($10,000 × $\frac{3}{10}$ × $\frac{9}{12}$).		$3,250
d $11,000 × 50% × $\frac{9}{12}$.	$4,125	
($11,000 − $4,125) × 50%.		$3,437.50

2	*General Journal*		
a	Cash	4,000	
	Accumulated Depreciation	1,800	
	Loss on Disposal of Machinery	200	
	Machinery		6,000
b	Cash	3,500	
	Accumulated Depreciation	2,700	
	Gain on Disposal of Machinery		200
	Machinery		6,000
c	Machinery	7,300	
	Accumulated Depreciation	3,600	
	Machinery		6,000
	Cash		4,900

3 Average earnings $4,000,000 × .20)...... $ 800,000
Excess earnings ($1,040,000 − $800,000).. $ 240,000
Goodwill ($240,000 ÷ .25)............ $ 960,000
Price offered ($4,000,000 + $960,000)... $4,960,000

FICA tax, **b** federal unemployment insurance tax, **c** state unemployment compensation tax. **8** $13,200, 6%. **9** W-2, Director of Internal Revenue. **10 a** FICA Tax Payable, **b** Federal Unemployment Tax Payable, **c** State Unemployment Tax Payable, **d** Liability for Income Tax Withheld.

CHAPTER 13

True or False

1 F **2** T **3** F **4** F **5** T **6** F **7** F **8** F **9** T
10 F **11** T **12** T **13** F **14** F **15** T **16** F **17** F
18 F **19** T **20** F

Completion Statements

1 Decrease. **2** Loss, $50,000. **3** Increases, decreases. **4** 100,000. **5 a** Mortgages payable, **b** lease obligations, **c** liabilities under pension plans. **6 a** Social security taxes, **b** federal and state income taxes withheld, **c** other deductions such as union dues, insurance premiums, etc. **7 a**

Multiple Choice

1 b **2** c **3** c **4** a **5** a **6** b **7** b **8** c **9** c
10 d

Solutions to Exercises

1 a $10,000 ($600,000 × 5% × $\frac{4}{12}$)
b The discount amounted to $5,800 ($604,200 − $600,000 − $10,000)
c $15,000 ($600,000 × 5% × $\frac{6}{12}$)
d $10,000 ($600,000 × 5% × $\frac{4}{12}$)
e $5,500 [$5,800 less amortization of $50 ($5,800 ÷ 116) per month for six months]
f $15,300 (interest on $600,000 at 5% for six months, $15,000, plus the amortization of discount for six months, $300).

2

	1976	General Journal			
a	July 1	Cash	604,200		
		Discount on Bonds Payable	5,800		
		Bonds Payable		600,000	
		Bond Interest Payable		10,000	
		To record issuance of bonds.			
b	Sept. 1	Bond Interest Payable	10,000		
		Bond Interest Expense	5,000		
		Cash		15,000	
		To record payment of interest for six months, including			
		$10,000 which was accrued on date bonds were issued.			
	1	Bond Interest Expense	100		
		Discount on Bonds Payable		100	
		To amortize discount for July and August at $50 per			
		month ($5,800 ÷ 116).			
c	Dec. 31	Bond Interest Expense	10,000		
		Bond Interest Payable		10,000	
		To accrue interest for four months.			
	31	Bond Interest Expense	200		
		Discount on Bonds Payable		200	
		To amortize discount for four months at $50 per			
		month.			

3	1977	General Journal			
a	Jan. 31	Manufacturing Wages	6,700		
		Sales Salaries	1,500		
		Administrative Salaries	1,800		
		FICA Tax Payable		600	
		Liability for Income Tax Withheld		1,350	
		Accrued Payroll		8,050	
		To record payroll for January.			
b	Jan. 31	Payroll Taxes Expense	920		
		FICA Tax Payable		600	
		State Unemployment Tax Payable		270	
		Federal Unemployment Tax Payable		50	
		To record employer's payroll taxes for January.			

4

	Plan A (Common stock only)	Plan B (Common and preferred stock)	Plan C (Common stock and bonds)
Earnings, before interest and income taxes.....	$800,000	$800,000	$800,000
Less: Interest on bonds, 7% on $5 million......			350,000
Earnings before income taxes...............	$800,000	$800,000	$450,000
Income taxes, 40%.....................	320,000	320,000	180,000
Net income........................	$480,000	$480,000	$270,000
Less: Dividend on preferred stock, 7% on $5 million.....................		350,000	
Net income available for common stock........	$480,000	$130,000	$270,000
Number of shares of common stock outstanding	1,000,000	500,000	500,000
Net income per share of common stock........	$ 0.48	$ 0.26	$ 0.54

CHAPTER 14

True or False

1 T **2** F **3** T **4** F **5** T **6** T **7** T **8** T **9** F
10 T **11** F **12** F **13** T **14** F **15** T **16** F **17** T
18 F **19** F **20** T **21** T **22** F **23** T **24** T **25** T
26 T

Multiple Choice

1 d **2** d **3** b **4** b **5** c **6** b **7** c **8** b **9** d

Completion Statements

1 a American Institute of Certified Public Accountants, **b** American Accounting Association, **c** Securities and Exchange Commission. **2** Going-concern. **3** Objectivity, consistency, disclosure. **4** Cost, current market. **5** Audit, opinion, fairness. **6 a** During production, **b** when production is complete, **c** when the sale is made, **d** when cash is collected from customers. **7** Purchasing power, decreases. **8** Common dollar.

Solutions to Exercises

1

	Assets	Liabilities	Owners' Equity
a	NE	NE	NE
b	D	NE	D
c	NE	NE	NE
d	I	NE	I
e	NE	NE	NE
f	NE	NE	NE
g	I	NE	I
h	D	NE	D

2

Case	Purchasing Power Gain	Purchasing Power Loss	Net Gain (or Loss)
a		$10,000	$(10,000)
b	$5,000	5,000	0
c	9,000		9,000

a $10,000 loss (holding cash of $100,000 while prices increased by 10%).

b No net gain or loss (loss of $5,000 from holding monetary assets is offset by the gain of $5,000 from owing money during a period of inflation).

c $9,000 gain (owing $90,000 while prices increased by 10%).

3

X CO.
Common Dollar Balance Sheet
End of Month

Assets	a	b	c
Cash..................................	$100,000	$ 10,000	
Accounts receivable...................		40,000	
Inventory.............................		27,500	$ 55,000
Equipment............................		27,500	55,000
Total assets.....................	$100,000	$105,000	$110,000

Liabilities & Stockholders' Equity			
Liabilities............................		$ 50,000	$ 90,000
Capital stock.........................	$ 88,000	11,000	5,500
Retained earnings....................	12,000	44,000	14,500
Total liabilities & stockholders' equity..	$100,000	$105,000	$110,000

CHAPTER 15

Multiple Choice

1 d **2** b **3** b **4** c **5** b **6** a **7** c **8** d

True or False

1 F **2** T **3** T **4** F **5** T **6** T **7** F **8** F **9** F
10 T **11** T **12** F **13** T **14** F **15** T **16** F **17** T
18 T **19** F **20** F

Completion Statements

1 Financial position, sources, uses, working capital. **2** Cash flow. **3** Declaration, use, source, use. **4** Added, net income, provided by operations. **5** Noncurrent. **6** Current. **7** Accrual, cash. **8** Decrease, increase, increase.

Solutions to Exercises

1

Net income.............................		$130,000
Add: Depreciation expense..............		40,000
Amortization of patents............		5,000
Subtotal..........................		$175,000
Less: Gain on sale of plant assets		
(net of taxes)..........	$20,000	
Amortization of premium on		
bonds payable.........	2,500	22,500
Working capital provided by operations...		$152,500

Note: The entire proceeds (including the gain) from the sale of plant assets should be reported as a nonoperating source of funds. Interest revenue, accrued salaries and wages expense, and income tax expense are properly included in the determination of net income since each of these items either increased or decreased working capital.

2

FERN CORPORATION

Statement of Changes in Financial Position

For Year Ended December 31, Year 2

Sources of working capital:

  Operations:

    Income before extraordinary

      items ($175,000 +

      $30,000 − $20,000). $185,000

    Add: Expenses not requiring

      use of current funds—

      depreciation.   25,000

    Total working capital

      provided by operations. $210,000

  Sale of land.   60,000

    Total sources of working

      capital. $270,000

Uses of working capital:

  Purchase of equipment. $84,000

  Declaration of cash dividend. . .   42,500

    Total uses of working capital   126,500

Increase in working capital. $143,500

d

Z COMPANY

Statement of Changes in Financial Position

For Current Year

Uses of working capital:

  Purchase of plant and

    equipment. $100,000

  Retirement of bonds payable.   20,000

  Payment of dividends.   35,000

    Total uses of working capital $155,000

Sources of working capital:

  Operations:

    Net income. $80,000

    Add: Depreciation expense.   15,000

    Total working capital pro-

      vided by operations.   95,000

Decrease in working capital. . . . . $ 60,000

3 **a** $275,000 − $45,000 = $230,000

  b $275,000 − $105,000 = $170,000

  c $230,000 − $170,000 = $(60,000) Decrease

e

Z COMPANY

Conversion of Income Statement from Accrual to Cash Basis

For Current Year

	Income Statement (Accrual Basis)	Add (Deduct)	Cash Basis
Net sales.	$800,000		
Add: Decrease in accounts receivable.		$20,000	$820,000
Cost of goods sold.	490,000		
Add: Increase in inventory.		10,000	
Less: Increase in accounts payable.		(65,000)	435,000
Gross profit on sales.	$310,000		$385,000
Expenses.	230,000		
Add: Decrease in accrued liabilities.		$ 5,000	
Less: Depreciation expense.		(15,000)	220,000
Net income.	$ 80,000		
Cash flow from operations.			$165,000

f

Z COMPANY
Cash Flow Statement
For Current Year

Cash receipts:

Cash flow from operations—		
see *e* above....................		$165,000
Sale of marketable securities..........		10,000
Total cash receipts.................		$175,000
Cash payments:		
Purchase of plant and		
equipment...............	$100,000	
Retirement of bonds payable..	20,000	
Payment of dividends........	35,000	
Total cash payments..............		155,000
Increase in cash during the year		$ 20,000

Completion Statements

1 Dollar, percentage, component percentages, ratios. *2 a* Short-term creditors, *b* long-term creditors, *c* preferred stockholders, *d* common stockholders. *3* Price-earnings ratio. *4* Equity ratio. *5 a* $150,000; *b* $50,000; *c* $75,000. *6* Long-term creditors, income from operations, interest expense. *7* Return on assets, low. *8* Inventory, inventory turnover.

Multiple Choice

1 c 2 d 3 d 4 a 5 c 6 d 7 b 8 b 9 c 10 d

CHAPTER 16

True or False

1 T *2* F *3* T *4* T *5* T *6* F *7* F *8* T *9* F
10 F *11* F *12* T *13* F *14* F *15* T *16* T *17* T
18 T *19* T *20* F

Solutions to Exercises

1

GOLDSTREAM COMPANY
Comparative Balance Sheet

Assets	Year 2	Year 1	Increase (or Decrease) Amount	Percentage
Current assets..................	$150,000	$120,000	$ 30,000	25%
Investments....................	160,000	80,000	80,000	100%
Plant and equipment (net).........	360,000	300,000	60,000	20%
Intangibles.....................	80,000	100,000	(20,000)	(20)%
Total assets..................	$750,000	$600,000	$150,000	25%
Liabilities & Stockholders' Equity				
Current liabilities................	$ 76,000	$ 80,000	$ (4,000)	(5)%
Long-term debt..................	116,000	100,000	16,000	16%
Capital stock, $5 par............	250,000	200,000	50,000	25%
Retained earnings................	308,000	220,000	88,000	40%
Total liabilities & stockholders' equity.....................	$750,000	$600,000	$150,000	25%

2 a $280,000 by $105,000
  b $140,000 by $105,000
  c $800,000 by $60,000 [($50,000 + $70,000) ÷ 2]
  d $490,000 by $135,000 [($140,000 + $130,000) ÷ 2]
  e $150,000 by $7,000
  f $91,000 by $657,500 [($700,000 + $615,000) ÷ 2]
  g $515,000 by $700,000

  h $84,000 by $492,500 [($515,000 + $470,000) ÷ 2]
  i $84,000 by 60,000
  j $42 by $1.40
  k $0.65 by $42
  l $515,000 by 60,000
  m $310,000 by $800,000
  n $160,000 by $800,000

3	Transaction or Event	Ratio	Effect
a	Purchased inventory on open account.	Quick ratio	−
b	A larger physical volume of goods was sold at reduced prices.	Gross profit percentage	−
c	Declared a cash dividend of $1 per share.	Current ratio	−
d	An uncollectible account receivable was written off against the allowance account.	Current ratio	NE
e	Issued additional shares of common stock and used proceeds to retire long-term debt.	Rate earned on total assets (before interest and income taxes)	NE
f	Distributed a 20% stock dividend on common stock.	Earnings per share of common stock	−
g	Operating income increased 25%; interest expense increased 10%.	Times interest charges earned	+
h	During period of rising prices, company changed from fifo to lifo method of inventory pricing.	Inventory turnover	+
i	Paid previously declared cash dividend.	Debt ratio	−
j	Issued shares of common stock in exchange for plant assets.	Equity ratio	+

CHAPTER 17

Completion Statements

1 Individuals, corporations, estates, trusts. 2 Income, sales, property, excise. 3 Information. 4 Itemize deductions, standard deduction, personal exemption. 5 Interest, taxes, contributions, medical expenses, casualty losses, production, income. 6 Constructively. 7 Income tax allocation.

True or False

1 T 2 F 3 T 4 T 5 F 6 T 7 F 8 T 9 T
10 F 11 F 12 T 13 T 14 F 15 F 16 T 17 F
18 T 19 F 20 T

Multiple Choice

1 a 2 c 3 d 4 c 5 d 6 c 7 d 8 d 9 b

Solutions to Exercises

1
ROBERT AND BETTY HILL
Computation of Taxable Income for 19___

Gross income:		
Salary...	$18,500	
Dividends ($580 — $200)............................	380	
Interest on savings account........................	320	
Net long-term capital gain ($8,000 — $4,200).............	3,800	$23,000
Deduction to arrive at adjusted gross income:		
Long-term capital gain deduction (50% of $3,800 reported in gross income)......................................		1,900
Adjusted gross income..		$21,100
Deductions from adjusted gross income:		
Itemized deductions:		

Sales taxes, including tax on new car...........	$ 400		
State income taxes paid.....................	300		
Contributions..............................	300		
Property taxes on residence and vacant lot.......	650		
Interest on mortgage and personal loan.........	1,320		
Medical expenses, $950 less $633 (3% of $21,100)	317		
Subscription to investment advisory service......	100		
Gasoline taxes..............................	60	$ 3,447	
Personal Exemptions (8 × $750).....................	6,000	9,447	
Taxable income..		$11,653	

2

Income before income taxes			$200,000
Add: Long-term capital loss (not deductible)..............	$ 8,000		
Amortization of goodwill (not deductible)..............	5,000	13,000	
Subtotal			$213,000
Less: 85% of $20,000 (dividends from other corporations)...	$17,000		
Interest received on municipal bonds (not taxable)........	4,500	21,500	
Taxable income			$191,500

3

Year	(a) Taxable Income	(b) Income Taxes, 40%	(a) — (b) Net Income
1	$10,000	$ 4,000	$ 6,000
2	70,000	28,000	42,000
3	20,000	8,000	12,000